Migrants to the Coasts

Migrants to the Coasts

Livelihood, Resource Management and Global Change in the Philippines

JAMES F. EDER
Arizona State University

 Case Studies on Contemporary Social Issues:
John A. Young, Series Editor

 **WADSWORTH**
CENGAGE Learning

Australia • Brazil • Japan • Korea • Mexico • Singapore • Spain • United Kingdom • United States

WADSWORTH
CENGAGE Learning

Migrants to the Coasts: Livelihood, Resource Management and Global Change in the Philippines
James F. Eder

Executive Editor: Marcus Boggs

Acquisitions Editor: Lin Marshall Gaylord

Assistant Editor: Liana Monari

Editorial Assistant: Paige Leeds

Marketing Manager: Meghan Pease

Marketing Assistant: Mary Anne Payumo

Marketing Communications Manager: Tami Strang

Project Manager, Editorial Production: Samen Iqbal

Creative Director: Rob Hugel

Art Director: Caryl Gorska

Print Buyer: Paula Vang

Permissions Editor: Bob Kauser

Production Service: Jill Wolf, Buuji

Copy Editor: Robin Gold

Cover Image: James F. Eder

Compositor: Integra

For product information and technology assistance, contact us at **Cengage Learning Customer & Sales Support, 1-800-354-9706**.
For permission to use material from this text or product, submit all requests online at **cengage.com/permissions**. Further permissions questions can be e-mailed to **permissionrequest@cengage.com**.

Library of Congress Control Number:

Student Edition:
ISBN-13: 978-0-495-09524-8
ISBN-10: 0-495-09524-9

Wadsworth
10 Davis Drive
Belmont, CA 94002-3098
USA

Cengage Learning is a leading provider of customized learning solutions with office locations around the globe, including Singapore, the United Kingdom, Australia, Mexico, Brazil, and Japan. Locate your local office at **international.cengage.com/region**.

Cengage Learning products are represented in Canada by Nelson Education, Ltd.

For your course and learning solutions, visit **academic.cengage.com**.

Purchase any of our products at your local college store or at our preferred online store **www.ichapters.com**.

Printed in Canada
1 2 3 4 5 6 7 12 11 10 09 08

*To Palawan's coastal dwellers and to those
who work with them to build a more sustainable way of life*

Brief Contents

Contents

List of Figures

Foreword

ABOUT THE SERIES

This book explores the practical applications of anthropology in understanding and addressing problems faced by human societies around the world. Each case study examines an issue of socially recognized importance in the historical, geographical, and cultural context of a particular region of the world, while adding comparative analysis to highlight the local effects of globalization and the global dimensions of the issue. The authors write with a readable narrative style and include reference to their own participation, roles, and responsibilities in the communities they study. Their engagement with people goes beyond observation and research, as they explain and sometimes illustrate from personal experience how their work has implications for advocacy, community action, and policy formation. The authors demonstrate how anthropological investigations can build our knowledge of human societies and at the same time provide the basis for fostering community empowerment, resolving conflicts, and pursuing social justice.

ABOUT THE AUTHOR

James Eder received his PhD in anthropology from the University of California, Santa Barbara, and is currently Professor of Anthropology in the School of Human Evolution & Social Change at Arizona State University. His interests in the Philippines trace to 3 years he spent there as a Peace Corps Volunteer, teaching high school biology and adult literacy on Palawan Island. Since then, Jim has returned to Palawan numerous times for a total of 6 years of anthropological fieldwork. His research interests include the subsistence activities of the Batak, a foraging people of the island's forested interior, and the interplay of economic change and social inequality in frontier farming communities. Jim's previous books include *Who Shall Succeed? Agricultural Development and Social Inequality on a Philippine Frontier, On the Road to Tribal Extinction: Depopulation, Deculturation, and Adaptive Well-being among the Batak of the Philippines,* and *A Generation Later: Household Strategies and Economic Change in the Rural Philippines.* He first became interested in fishing communities during his travels by fishing boat to some of the many small islands of the Palawan region.

ABOUT THIS CASE STUDY

This case study explores the impact of globalization on environmental and human well-being in the coastal zone of Palawan Island in the Philippines. The reader will learn about histories, livelihoods, gender roles, socioeconomic hierarchies and the interdependency of fishing and farming in communities whose members are of different ethnic backgrounds and who originally settled or recently migrated to this region. Each of these communities has a unique pattern for using resources with a corresponding impact on the environment. Globalization affects local patterns of resource exploitation by causing population growth and introducing technologies and market forces that intensify destructive kinds of resource use. The movement to conserve the natural environment also has a global reach, as illustrated by an unsuccessful attempt to establish a series of marine protected areas in the municipality of San Vicente. The author bases his assessment of this failure on interviews conducted in four of the ten communities in San Vicente, and on a comparative analysis of similar projects in the Philippines and elsewhere. Although officials cited technical problems, the failure to establish viable marine protected areas was primarily the lack of real local participation and inattention to people's daily needs in pursuing their livelihoods. As infrastructure and the social environment change, some households on their own find new ways to make a living that reduce the pressure on marine resources. The author concludes by suggesting that conservation policies and projects have greater chance for success by facilitating appropriate new ways of making a living.

John A. Young, Series Editor

Preface

For those concerned about the health of the world's coastal ecosystems and the well-being of the millions of people who rely upon them for their livelihood, the news from coastal Southeast Asia is sobering. Such catch phrases as "the rush of poverty to the coasts" and "too many people chasing too few fish" only begin to suggest the environmental damage caused by excessive human exploitation of the region's coastal resources during the past 50 years. Dwindling fish stocks reflect relentless destruction of coral reefs, sea grass beds, and mangrove forests. As the health of Southeast Asia's coastal ecosystems has deteriorated, the livelihoods of millions of the region's inhabitants have suffered apace; fish catches are everywhere in decline, and earning a satisfactory living from other coastal resources has grown increasingly difficult, even as the numbers of coastal dwellers continue to grow. A pressing global need for biodiversity conservation and an insistent local demand for food and income security seem to pull in opposite directions.

How did such a state of affairs come about, and why should Americans be concerned about it? For most readers of this book, Southeast Asia may seem an exotic and faraway place, but increasingly, it is neither. Romantic images of the region aside, the concerns of most of Southeast Asia's ordinary rural inhabitants are not unlike our own. These concerns center on such everyday matters as how to earn a living and to prosper in a world of diminishing natural resources and greater economic competition, and how to educate and secure a better future for our children. A web of global interconnections has drawn Southeast Asia closer to us than it might first appear. Whether as beachgoers, as scuba-diving ecotourists, or as patrons of upscale restaurants with "live fish" on the menus, hundreds of thousands of Western tourists affect the region's coasts annually. If you are a tropical fish fancier or have purchased any shrimp at your local supermarket, there is a good chance you have become a consumer of coastal Southeast Asian resources without even leaving home.

The unprecedented demands that development and population growth now place on coastal resources are well known to scholars, policy makers, and a growing proportion of the general public. Marine biologists have documented the decline of fish stocks and the destruction of coral reefs. Ecologists have studied the destruction of shellfish habitat, sea grass beds, and mangrove forests. Social scientists have researched the role of human activities in all of these changes to better understand their causes. Meanwhile, throughout coastal Southeast Asia, government agencies and nongovernmental organizations are attempting to arrest or reverse these alarming trends with a variety of coastal resource management projects that draw financial support from the international environmentalist community. One goal of such projects is to foster local participation in biodiversity conservation initiatives.

The track record of these coastal resource management projects has been mixed. Scattered local successes in some communities continue to be negated elsewhere by illegal commercial fishing in municipal waters, by continued use of destructive fishing techniques, and by the lack of alternative livelihood opportunities in coastal areas. Would-be conservers of Southeast Asia's coastal zone resources are still trying to get things right.

Answers to Southeast Asia's coastal resource dilemmas have proven elusive, but I firmly believe that answers exist. I believe that anthropologists can find answers by examining in detail the successes and failures of past projects, by listening more carefully to what local people themselves have to say about how best to strike a balance between livelihood and conservation, and by a holistic approach that focuses on all human activities in the coastal zone, rather than just on fishing.

I will show in this volume how anthropology can contribute to biodiversity conservation and better human livelihoods in the coastal zone. At the same time, I will also show that the local residents of coastal Southeast Asia—in particular those who reside in San Vicente in the Philippines—are not "exotic others" but people who attempt to cope with global changes much as we do. Knowing when to see differences with others and when to see similarities is one of the central challenges of cross-cultural understanding, and I shall have something to say about that as well.

This book grew out of a field research project in the Philippines that began in spring 2002, with the support of a Fulbright Award from the Council for the International Exchange of Scholars and a sabbatical leave from Arizona State University (ASU). I continued the project with a series of return visits, during the summers of 2003, 2005, and 2006, the last visit supported by an A. T. Steele Travel Grant from ASU's Center for Asian Studies. Also I would like to acknowledge the generous assistance of two ASU undergraduate students, Noah Theriault and Melanie Tluczek, who helped me to tabulate and think through my field data. Thanks are also due to University of Hawaii Press for permission to use, in altered form, material that originally appeared in *a Generation Later: Household Strategies and Economic Change in the Rural Philippines*. For their assistance during fieldwork or for helpful comments on the manuscript, I thank Meng Amihan, Rebecca Austin, Regino Balofiños, Jovita Borres, Maribel Buñi, Romeo Cabungcal, Dante Dalabajan, Michael Fabinyi, Katherine Jack, Flora Leucadio, Inocencio Magellanes, Wilson Pambid, Noah Theriault, Lilibeth

Uapal, Jess Velete, and John Young. I owe many debts of gratitude to the people and families in San Vicente, but I particularly want to acknowledge the hospitality and kindness of Boy and Eden Collado, Tony and Winnie Manook, Bruce Lee and Russielle Prudenciado, and Abraham and Leah Uapal.

1

✳

Southeast Asian Coastal Ecosystems in Distress

S ometimes it seems that everyone in the world wants something from coastal Southeast Asia. Indigenous peoples and other long-time local residents want to maintain their traditional fishing-based livelihoods while securing the future well-being of their children. Migrant fishing people, some from hinterland regions and some from other coasts, seek new livelihoods of their own and, in the process, increase collection pressures on local fish stocks. Both long-time local residents and recently arrived migrants often lose out to large commercial fishing boats intruding on local waters from afar with their technologically modern and highly efficient gear. Members of the international environmentalist community want to see Southeast Asia's coastal resources conserved for their wealth of biodiversity even as millions of global consumers are anxious to consume the fish, shrimp, and other resources of coastal ecosystems. The result of these competing pressures has been a dreary combination of coral reef destruction, mangrove deforestation, diminished fish stocks, and growing economic hardship for the millions of people who rely on the resources of coastal Southeast Asia to make their livings and support their families. Although these are extraordinarily challenging problems, they are not insurmountable problems. As I shall show in this book, anthropology has much to contribute toward their solution.

My own efforts in this regard began modestly, on a fine spring day on a beautiful tropical beach in San Vicente, on Palawan Island in the Philippines—the idealized palm-lined, beach paradise of many Americans' daydreams. However, this beach held a surprise for me. Rather than encountering a few lone fishermen here and there going about their work, I instead discovered a boisterous throng of people, mostly women and children, engaged in what for me was an unfamiliar activity: beach seining. All up and down the beach, teams of people were pulling on long lines, slowly drawing in even longer nets that a few hours earlier had been set hundreds of meters out to sea (see Figure 1.1). As they worked together to pull in their nets, all eyes were seemingly on me. How does one meet two hundred

1

Courtesy of James F. Eder

FIGURE 1.1 Beach seiners at New Agutaya

strangers all at once? I had hoped for a low key, one-on-one encounter with a willing fisherman, and I was not prepared for such a large group. As I approached, I heard the predictable calls of "hey Joe, where are you going?" I could also overhear ribald joking at my expense among the older women, some of it alarmingly explicit. Things improved marginally once I was able to strike up a light conversation in a local language with a few of the friendlier-looking seiners, but this only made me an object of greater curiosity. I suddenly found myself unable to explain in any satisfactory way why I was there and, much to everyone's amusement, I could not even properly pronounce the name of the beach. (The name of the beach is *Pinagmangalokan,* and I still trip when I attempt to say it.)

Being an anthropologist had gotten me into this trouble, and it got me back out. I wanted to understand what they were doing even as I was eager to deflect attention from myself. Because they needed to get back to work and I saw room on one of the pull lines, I asked if I could join them. I did "participant observation" the rest of the morning. I pulled and pulled on the line, along with everyone else, and by mid-day I had made some friends, learned some things, and earned a small basket of fish (my share of the catch) for my efforts—all in all, not bad for a morning's fieldwork.

The following day I experienced a mildly embarrassing sequel to this adventure. During a visit to the municipal hall to meet the mayor and other town officials, I discovered that the beach seining I had so enthusiastically embraced was illegal. The nets damage sea grass beds and bring in a lot of "by-catch"—small fish that otherwise would have grown bigger or that would not be consumed by humans. Fortunately for me, and for reasons I discuss in this book, the ban on beach seining was not yet being enforced, and I suffered nothing worse than good-natured teasing about my ignorance of the very matters I had come to study. My momentary, "what am I doing here?" crisis of confidence on the beach the first day and the teasing on the second day soon faded into the past, but my experiences on both days have long stuck in my mind as reminders of how preparations for anthropological fieldwork are never as complete as we might like them to be.

What past experiences, research interests, and other considerations brought me to that beach that day? On the scholarly side, I have long been drawn to the study of internal, rural-to-rural migration in Southeast Asia, which typically involves the voluntary movement of individuals and households from regions of economic hardship and political unrest to frontier regions of greater economic opportunity. I also have an abiding interest in rural development and in how the benefits of development are shared (or not) among the region's rural poor. And finally, as public concern about environmental degradation in Southeast Asia has mounted, I have been attracted to the study of programs designed to better manage the region's dwindling natural resources. Migration, development, poverty, and environmental degradation all intersect in the coastal zones of the region. Addressing these interrelated issues is critical to the well-being of the region's millions of inhabitants.

On a more personal side, a story from the past helps explain why I choose to pursue these questions in the Philippines rather than some other place, and how I choose to approach the questions. I first went to the Philippines as a recent college graduate and for reasons quite unrelated to anthropology. I had joined the Peace Corps, and after having majored in biology at the California Institute of Technology, I went to teach the subject at the high school in Puerto Princesa City, the capital of Palawan province, today a bustling urban center but then still a sleepy provincial town. (The Province of Palawan consists of Palawan Island and numerous smaller islands nearby.) Transformative life experiences in the Peace Corps prompted a shift in my academic interests from biology to anthropology. Since that time, Palawan has been my life's work, and my second home.

During more than a dozen return visits to Palawan and many more years of residence, I have studied such topics as the emergence of social inequality in a frontier farming community and the hardships that a small group of forest-dwelling indigenous people has endured as they have been incorporated into wider Philippine economy and society. I have learned about hunting and gathering, shifting cultivation, truck gardening, tree farming, kinship systems, and indigenous religious beliefs and practices of people on Palawan. And over the years, I have traveled extensively on the island, a marvelous place of considerable natural beauty, as photos included in this volume will show. From these travels and periodic encounters with my former high school students—some now farmers or fishermen, and others now government officials, teachers, and professionals—I have become intimately familiar with the everyday lives of "Palaweños."

Many other outsiders went to Palawan before me. Though the island remains in important ways relatively isolated and, for some, still an exotic destination, for centuries Palawan has been enmeshed in a network of global connections. The currently popular "last frontier" imagery surrounding Palawan partially obscures these connections, about which much remains to be discovered. After almost 500 years, Palawan is still being discovered and rediscovered.

In 1522, the remnants of Ferdinand Magellan's expedition to circumnavigate the globe put ashore briefly in Palawan, en route to the Spice Islands. Antonio Pigafetta, Magellan's chronicler, wrote enthusiastically about the abundance of Palawan's resources and the prosperity of its residents. For centuries, however, Palawan only received periodic mention in European historical records. Despite Spain's 350-year colonization of the Philippines, it never wrested full control over the island away from Muslim peoples emanating from the Malay Sultanates of Sulu and Brunei in the south, and Palawan received few European visitors. James Brooke, the British adventurer who became Rajah of Sarawak during the 1840s, briefly visited southern Palawan and gave Brookes Point, a town at the southern end of the island, its name. The first detailed descriptive account of life in Palawan by a European appeared as late as 1883, written by the French explorer Alfred Marche (Marche 1970).

Since the time of Marche's visit, whether for business, tourism, or some other purpose, Western visitors have continued to make their way to Palawan. Just south of San Vicente, on Ulugan Bay, one can still see the ruins of a large house built by a Frenchman in the 1920s. Why was he there? No one seems to know. When I first arrived in Palawan, the few Americans in town included several former soldiers from World War II who had chosen to remain behind and make a new life in the Philippines. One was in the road-building business; he had previously hunted crocodiles. A couple of years ago, I heard from a German historian specializing in the Philippines whom I had previously met at a conference. He had run across a letter dated in 1937 and written by a German evidently living at the time in an isolated part of southern Palawan; this historian wondered if I could find out more about the German on Palawan and why he was there. (I was unable to learn more.)

In more recent years, the glossy in-flight magazines of Philippine Airlines have regularly featured Palawan and the provincial government of Palawan has attempted to market Palawan as an ecotourism destination, where "every island is an adventure." Catholicism and Islam have existed for centuries in Palawan. Protestant influences are newer, but still well established—a Baptist missionary was among the few Americans I encountered when I first arrived more than 30 years ago. Today a towering Latter-day Saints (LDS, also known as Mormon) church is under construction in Puerto Princesa City, and in recent years, young American L.D.S. missionaries have began to make their own ways to Palawan.

In reflecting on these and other connections between Palawan and the "outside world" and observing the growing numbers of visitors to the island and the variety of their activities, my understandings of change and development in Palawan and my personal relationships with those whose lives I study have evolved apace. I do not claim to know everything there is to know about Palawan or its people. Quite the contrary, mine is a classic case of, "the more I know, the more I realize I don't know." My reflections on what I did not know prompted me to undertake the research that led to this book.

I did not know very much about fishing. I had traveled extensively in and around Palawan on various kinds of fishing boats, and occasionally I had gone fishing myself, but I lacked a satisfactory understanding of how fishing and coastal resource use fit into the larger picture of the settlement and development of Palawan. The tens of thousands of fishing people who inhabit coastal Palawan had somehow remained outside of my land-based and agriculture-oriented frame of reference. All my previous research had been limited to people who hunted and gathered in the forests or pursued various forms of agriculture in more settled areas. In the Philippines, fishing and farming, and fishers and farmers, have seldom been studied together. Anthropological studies of farming and of farming peoples cover such topics as pioneer settlement and forest clearance, agricultural intensification, and patterns of labor use, whereas anthropological studies of fishing and of fishing peoples cover such topics as fishing strategies, catch sharing, and marketing arrangements. Beyond anthropology, fishing and farming are typically the subjects of different disciplines altogether (for example, marine biology in the case of fishing and agronomy and agricultural economics in the case of farming). I had been party to this scholarly division of labor, but I had also begun to appreciate that when viewed against the reality of the everyday rural Philippines, the scholarly literatures on these two ways of life are more separate than are the life ways themselves. In coastal regions, fishing and farming are routinely found side-by-side, not only in the same communities but even in the same households. Hence, my first motive in undertaking this research was to better understand fishing and fishing peoples in Palawan and to explore how their lives and livelihoods relate to those of their agriculturally oriented neighbors in the coastal zone.

My second motive was that I had come to appreciate Palawan's cultural diversity. Much of my understanding of the island's settlement and development was centered on the experiences and perspectives of one particular cultural group, the Cuyonon. Originating from the small island of Cuyo that lies to the east of Palawan Island in the Sulu Sea, the Cuyonon have played a major role in the history of the Palawan region. They figured prominently in the early settlement of Palawan, but they are only one of numerous migrant peoples during the last century who have cleared the coastal plains and portions of the island's interior for agricultural settlement, in the process partially displacing Palawan's indigenous peoples from their ancestral territories. In seeking to understand settler peoples, I had worked primarily with Cuyonon, and over time I came to embrace and accept their view of themselves as "first among equals" in Palawan's history. Though I can make a case for this view, it subtly marginalizes an increasingly large population of settlers who originate farther away in the Visayan Island region of the central Philippines. Tracing their origins to such islands as Cebu, Bohol, Leyte, and Negros, these migrant "Visayans" are clearly destined to play an increasingly important role in the island's future. I realized that I should set aside my Cuyonon-centered views about Palawan's settlement and development and seek out Visayans to engage them on their own terms and in one of their own languages—Cebuano (I'm still working on that part!).

A third motive was my desire to engage more directly than I had in my prior research important issues—environmental crisis, economic difficulty, social well-being—that affect us all. I have long cared deeply about these issues in Palawan, and much of my previous research there had been focused on various kinds of rural livelihoods and on how social inequality affected people's chances in life. I had routinely donated my books and other publications on these topics to the offices of the various government and nongovernmental organization (NGO) agencies in Palawan concerned with designing and implementing development projects. Although they always gratefully received my publications, and at least some government officials and NGO workers appeared to genuinely respect my research and what I had to say, I had come to appreciate that I had not framed or presented my findings in ways that they found useful in designing their own projects and programs. My third motive was to try harder than I had in the past to make my findings relevant to their own development-related activities. In short, I wanted to do a more applied anthropology than I had done in the past, an endeavor that more directly served the practical needs of people, communities, and organizations in society (Ervin 2005). With that end in mind, I look forward to my next visit to Palawan. There I will give copies of this book to the government officials and NGO staff members who work on resource management issues and were so helpful in my research. In this way, I will reciprocate for their help with my research. I also plan to seek opportunities for continued dialogue about coastal resource management with local decision-makers, now focused on how my recommendations in this book might be implemented, modified, or improved.

As I thought about how to proceed in view of these motives, I realized that after years of studying small rural communities I would now need to "scale up" my research to a larger geographical and social unit of study. Regarding the earlier theme of Palawan's global connections, I worried that an entirely local focus might miss crucial dimensions of the very topics I aimed to learn more about—coastal resource use and the lives and concerns of those who fished for a living, and how Visayan-speaking peoples figured in Palawan's settlement and development. I sought a framework for my research sufficiently large and bounded in a way that clearly placed the people whose lives I proposed to study on a global stage and explicitly recognized the network of global connections that today strongly affect local lives and livelihoods. At the same time, I did not want a framework so large that I would lose sight of local people and local processes of change. A municipality seemed an appropriately sized framework for study. Philippine municipalities contain ten to thirty or more local communities, and in Palawan, these communities can vary considerably in ethnic makeup and livelihood depending on their ecological circumstances and their histories of settlement. In addition, municipal governments are themselves important actors in Philippine development and serve as a kind of "gatekeeper" between the global and the local. For example, some of the global forces affecting local lives are, like the coastal resource management project considered in this volume, mediated through the apparatus of the municipal government.

I also realized that I would need to carefully consider the phenomenon of "globalization," and though I will have more to say about this process and its consequences in San Vicente in later chapters, here briefly is what it is about. Capital, people, goods, images, and ideologies today flow more freely around the world than ever before and draw more and more of the globe into webs of interconnection. The outcome has been "globalization," world-wide processes of change that reshape local conditions and local lives on an ever-intensifying scale (Inda and Rosaldo 2004: 2–4), resulting in what one observer has called a "compression of the world" (Robertson 1992: 8). Globalization has many dimensions and definitions, but central to the process for many scholars is the increased integration of various places and peoples into the world economy (Edelman and Haugerud 2005: 3). According to Riall Nolan,

> Globalization refers, in essence, to a coming together of the major components of world economic activity—including finance, production, information, technology—within an overarching market-driven framework. This framework now extends in one way or another into virtually every corner of the globe. The World Bank estimates that today, fewer than 10 percent of the world's workers remain disconnected from world markets. (2002: 228)

People and their resources have been drawn into global webs of economic interconnection. Resources once available primarily to local residents to support themselves are today increasingly within access of more powerful outsiders better positioned to exploit them. Economic globalization has many powerful economic and political proponents, but critics of the global economy as presently constituted argue that the benefits of globalization have accrued primarily to large corporations and to residents of the already developed countries, whereas the costs are disproportionately borne by the poor and relatively powerless residents of third world countries, who in turn suffer unemployment, exploitation of their labor, and erosion of the natural resources on which their livelihoods depend. This inequity is the result of "free trade" agreements and other currently popular government economic policies that open local markets to relentless and debilitating global competition.

For some such people, such as smallholding farmers in the third world, the primary impact of global trade agreements has been displacement or unemployment caused by the importation of agricultural goods produced more cheaply elsewhere. After Mexico, Canada, and the United States signed the North American Free Trade Agreement (NAFTA) in 1994, for example, cheap (and heavily subsidized) corn produced in the United States flooded Mexican markets, and Mexican corn farmers suffered a 50 percent reduction in the prices paid for their corn. Since NAFTA was signed, an estimated 1.5 million farmers in Mexico have left their lands to seek factory jobs in Mexican cities or to work as farm laborers in the United States (Elliott 2006: 150–151). More recently, chili peppers produced in China have begun to flood Mexican produce markets as well, and Mexican chili pepper producers have been suffering a similar fate.

Frequently, global forces have degraded the very resources upon which local residents depend to produce their goods or to otherwise make a living. For example, mineral development in Papua New Guinea, export-oriented shrimp mariculture in Honduras, and tourism development in Malawi have all filled national and multinational coffers while degrading and diminishing access to local common-property resources, reducing local food security, and undermining the ability of local residents to earn a living (Derman and Ferguson 1994; Johnston and Jorgensen 1994; Stonich 1994). The benefits and costs of economic growth and global change have been unequally distributed in Southeast Asia in particular, and this disparity is a major theme of studies of development in the region (e.g., Aragon 1997; Rigg 2003). Development has not been fair, and in Southeast Asia and elsewhere, growing numbers of scholars, journalists, and ordinary local residents have decried the human and environmental costs of current patterns of global economic growth and called for more socially just alternatives (see, e.g., Broad and Cavanagh 1993; Johnston 1994, 1997). The title of one recent book concerned with the human costs of corporate domination of the world economy, *Alternatives to Globalization: A Better World is Possible* (Cavanagh and Mander 2004), nicely captures the belief of these critics that the negative impacts of contemporary global economic forces are not inevitable and that different economic policies—if the political will could be found to implement them—could mitigate or even reverse these impacts.

The world's peoples are today laced together in networks of relationships that test our ability to comprehend them, much less to deal with them. This complexity poses a considerable challenge to anthropologists hoping to offer practical guidance on how to improve human well-being (Doughty 2005: 303). According to Paul Doughty, an applied anthropologist, we

> ... must be prepared to range back and forth between the local and the global and back again. In this context, understanding and coping with globalization means being able to apply a holistic perspective at various levels of analysis while being able to develop policy and programs based upon the strength of knowledge drawn from intimate case research. (2005: 303)

Why study San Vicente? I had never even been there, although for an anthropologist that is always part of its appeal. I will introduce the municipality of San Vicente and its local communities and inhabitants more formally in Chapter 2, but here let me say that I first learned of it years ago, while I was still teaching at the local high school in Puerto Princesa City. Several of my students were from San Vicente, and they spoke enthusiastically of its pristine beaches and abundant fish stocks. About this same time, a major logging operation began in San Vicente to extract some of the most valuable tropical hardwoods found on Palawan. For several decades, San Vicente grew rapidly in population, as migrants from throughout the Philippines—but particularly from the Visayan Island region—arrived to seek work either in the logging industry or in the fishing economy. When I began scouting for a research site in earnest, I learned that San Vicente had been selected along with five pilot sites elsewhere in the Philippines to participate in a large Coastal Resource Management Project (CRMP). Funded by the U.S. Agency for International Development (USAID) and administered by the Philippine government's Department of Environment and Natural Resources, this ambitious project aimed to work with municipal governments to implement a new and more effective approach to the management of coastal resources. Thus, San Vicente appeared a promising locale to conduct my research.

I did not begin my fieldwork that day on the beach with an already well-defined list of research questions. Rather, and as often happens in anthropological fieldwork, I arrived in the field with the general motives and research interests that I described earlier. As I became acquainted with both people and place, these interests evolved into questions, which in turn lent more focus to my research.

First, I asked about local livelihoods and patterns of resource use, and to what degree they vary within and between communities. An answer to this question required close-up and detailed ethnographic observation of fishing, farming, and other economic activities at various places within San Vicente. How I chose those places and how I collected such information are among the topics of Chapter 2, and in Chapter 4, I report what I found out about these matters during the course of my research.

My second question was, how are global forces experienced locally, particularly regarding how these forces affect the exploitation of coastal resources? I knew from previous research that various global demands had caused significant coastal resource depletion throughout Palawan. I also knew that some Palawan residents had benefited from global change, sometimes as local facilitators of resource degradation by outside interests, but that most had not benefited or were even being hurt. I did not know how the relationships between global demands and local resource use practices played out in San Vicente in particular, and this became my second question. To answer it required me to explore both the wider political economy of natural resource use in the Philippines, the subject of Chapter 3, and to continue my ethnographic study of local livelihoods and resource use, now focused on how these may have changed over time, a topic also included in Chapter 4.

From my prior research, I also knew that various government and nongovernmental agencies and programs were already attempting to do something to stem further degradation of coastal resources and help local residents to manage those resources on a more sustainable basis. One such effort, the CRMP noted earlier, had been implemented in San Vicente before my arrival, but as I was to learn, it had not been very successful. My third question hence became, why had this well-meaning, well-funded, and seemingly well-designed project produced few if any accomplishments? An answer to this question required careful attention to the design, implementation, and results of the project, viewed both from the perspective of the project implementers and from the perspective of local residents. The latter, the project's intended "beneficiaries," in turn varied among themselves in how they perceived and experienced the project, and this too required my attention. What the Coastal Resource Management Project intended to do, how local people responded to it, and my own evaluation of it all are the subjects of Chapter 5.

Fourth, my long-standing general interest and concern about the well-being of rural dwellers in the Philippines coalesced around the crucial need to develop more sustainable and remunerative ways to earn livings in the coastal zone. New ways of living were important not just on grounds of human well-being or social justice; they also might help relieve relentless and destructive pressures on San Vicente's remaining stocks of coastal resources and give local residents greater incentive to cooperate in the improved management of those resources. The term "alternative livelihoods" refers to these much-needed new ways of making a living in parts of the world suffering from excessive resource exploitation. I wondered how anthropology might help identify and develop alternative livelihoods most suitable for the inhabitants of San Vicente? My answers to this fourth question are found in Chapters 6 and 7.

These are not easy questions, and I knew that to engage them effectively I would need to investigate other matters well. I will let most of these come up later, but here I mention two topics that I knew from my previous research would prove particularly important. One is the prominent role of women in the Philippines in household economic affairs. Women are primarily responsible for the day-to-day management of household budgets, and they often take a lead role in developing and implementing new household economic activities. To have something useful to say about suitable new livelihoods in San Vicente, I would need to consider the role of women in present livelihoods and in setting household agendas.

The other topic I would need to investigate concerns the role of culture and ethnic identity in the actual use of coastal resources. San Vicente's residents come from various parts of the Philippines and have different languages and cultural traditions. What is the nature of these differences in cultural background, and how do they influence the views of local residents and their use of coastal resources? As an anthropologist, I believe that "culture matters," and for some anthropologists it might appear self-evident that the answer to this question should be "yes." I also knew that despite differences in geographical origin and language, the residents of San Vicente were culturally similar in many important respects. For this reason and because it is no less important for anthropologists than for others to periodically question their beliefs, I thought I should also consider the possibility that cultural differences might not figure at all in coastal resource use or that any such differences that did exist had been effectively "trumped" by ecological, economic, or political circumstances. Thus, I would need to ask questions such as these: Do all fishermen of similar economic means and in similar environments use the same gear and the same technique to catch fish, or do they differ in gear and technique depending on their cultural background?

As I seek answers to these and other questions in this book, I will also show how the lives and concerns of San Vicente's residents are intertwined with those of other people in other places. It has become a truism to declare that people in any particular place today live in a global society. Evidence for this proposition certainly exists in San Vicente—witness the ubiquitous cell phones and the growing popularity of satellite television, a phenomenon I will discuss in Chapter 6. However, evidence of globalization and interconnectedness is just half of the story. The other and more important half is to show how globalization matters. For example, how does interconnectedness with global markets affect how local residents earn their livings and use coastal resources? And how does membership in a global society influence the aspirations of local residents for their children or their notions about what kind of life is worth living?

These are the questions that anthropologists, with their holistic approach, are uniquely prepared to answer. As I offer my own answers in this volume, I will show that most residents of San Vicente are not benefiting from global inter-connections. The generalization that globalization has everywhere increased the disparities between those who "have" and those who "have not" may be a truism, but most San Vicente residents fall into the "have not" category, and this fact cannot be ignored by those who seek to enlist their assistance in making resource management projects succeed. Whatever else globalization has brought to San Vicente, it has been growing awareness among local residents of where they stand in the world, and growing awareness of social injustice in their own country.

2

※

San Vicente, a Coastal Philippine Municipality

The municipality of San Vicente lies on the northwest coast of Palawan Island facing the South China Sea (Figure 2.1) and consists of ten communities, one of which is also the municipal seat. San Vicente's total land area is 840,000 hectares and its population (according to the 2000 census) is 21,654 persons. Only a few poorly maintained gravel roads connect San Vicente with the national highway that runs up and down the east coast of the island. These roads accommodate several buses, freight trucks, and passenger vans that originate each day in Puerto Princesa City or in Roxas, a neighboring municipality on the east coast. Also connecting San Vicente with the outside world are boats that ply routes to the various islands of northern Palawan, to the Visayan Islands and infrequently to Manila. A small airport serves primarily to fly out live fish and secondarily to receive irregular passenger flights by an on-demand commuter airline based in Puerto Princesa City. For the most part, San Vicente is isolated and hard to reach, and local residents who travel to Roxas or Puerto Princesa City must spend the night there before returning home.

Basic services in San Vicente include a health clinic at the municipal seat and several community health stations, two-dozen elementary schools, and four high schools. San Vicente residents are still predominantly Catholic, but many other churches are also present, including Baptist, Pentecostal, Adventist, and *Iglesia ni Christo* (Church of Christ), a Philippines-based denomination. A municipal electrical grid serves the denser built-up areas between 6:00 and 10:00 P.M. each day. Here and there one finds stores, small restaurants, private "VHS" houses showing videos for a small entrance fee, and a couple of drinking establishments featuring karaoke and "videoke," where the lyrics for amateur singers appear on a TV screen (Figure 2.2).

San Vicente's ten communities lie in an irregular row along the coast, such that each community includes a stretch of coastline, a corresponding area of ocean out to the legally defined 15-kilometer municipal waters limit, and a

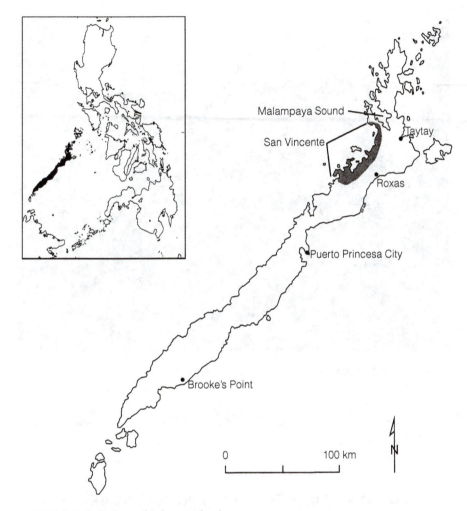

FIGURE 2.1 Map of Palawan Island

corresponding area of land, including a flat coastal portion cleared for settlement and a mountainous and forested interior portion (Figure 2.3). Various small islands, some inhabited, lie along the coast; each is also part of one of the ten communities. This geographic pattern suggests the characteristic, mixed "fishing and farming" economic base of San Vicente communities. Fishing with various kinds of equipment and various levels of capital investment occurs along the coast and around the small offshore islands, irrigated rice agriculture occurs in areas of the coastal plain favored by adequate water resources, and a mixed upland agriculture—corn, root crops, coconuts, bananas, and fruit trees—occurs elsewhere on the coastal plain and in the foothills. This geography facilitated my travel between communities. I could take the bus that twice daily plied a graded dirt road along the coastal plain, I could hire a small boat to run me up or down

FIGURE 2.2   Restaurant and karaoke bar in Alimanguan

the coast by sea, or I could walk along the beach—always an enjoyable but time-consuming option.

COASTAL ZONE HABITATS AND RESOURCES

The beach, the ocean, and the coastal plain are only the most visible components of the complex and resource-rich coastal ecosystem that San Vicente residents rely upon to make their livings. As an anthropologist hoping to make useful recommendations about how to better manage coastal resources, I had a lot to learn about this ecosystem and how local residents understood its workings, if others were to take my recommendations seriously. The ecosystem concept originated in biology, but anthropologists have adopted it to study human adaptation. Many resource managers use it to better understand human impacts on the environment. Most natural ecosystems are complex affairs, but the basic analytical concept is straight forward: within an ecosystem various organisms, including humans, interact with each other and with various components of the environment; the nature of these interactions are the subject of study. Some ecosystems, such as ponds, are relatively well bounded geographically, but others, including coastal and marine ecosystems, are more open. Coral reefs' ecosystems

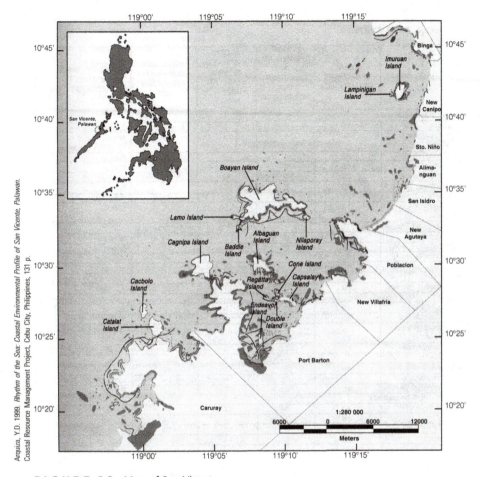

Arquiza, Y.D. 1999. *Rhythm of the Sea: Coastal Environmental Profile of San Vicente, Palawan.* Coastal Resource Management Project, Cebu City, Philippines, 131 p.

FIGURE 2.3 Map of San Vicente

may appear physically distinct, but fish and other resources move freely between coral reefs and neighboring habitats, as do the humans who rely upon these resources. San Vicente was a political unit embedded in a wider coastal ecosystem whose components and properties I tried to understand.

Marine Habitats and Resources

From the standpoint of human use, mangroves, sea grass beds, and coral reefs are the most important marine components of this wider coastal ecosystem. All serve as fish nurseries or foraging areas for food fish. Each component is itself an ecosystem, but each is also linked to the others by nutrient flows, predator-prey relations, and the movement of fish from one habitat to another during their life cycle (Figure 2.4). Coral reefs in particular are open systems whose well-being requires the influx of fresh water from terrestrial systems and inputs of nitrogen from nearby

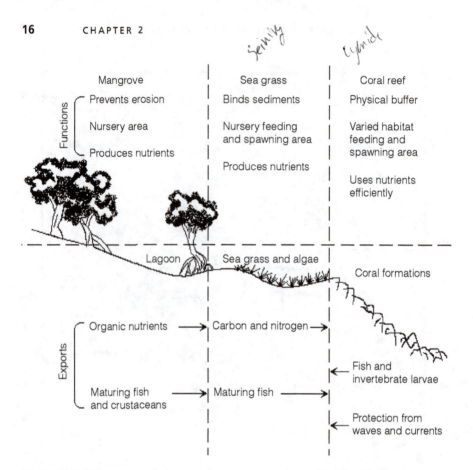

FIGURE 2.4 Linkages between mangrove, sea grass, and coral reef ecosystems

sea grass beds and mangroves. The open structure of coral reef communities thus requires holistic and integrated management approaches capable of taking these external linkages into account. If the larger coastal ecosystem is to remain healthy, so too must each component ecosystem upon which its health depends.

Coral reefs consist of masses of cemented calcium carbonate upon which living corals, known as polyps, attach themselves and build up over hundreds of years. Most common in the Philippines are so-called fringing reefs, formed under water on the outer edges of volcanic islands and islets, either directly attached to the shore, or more commonly, bordering the shore with an intervening shallow channel or lagoon. Organic nutrients and algae from mangroves and sea grass beds create a favorable habitat for hundreds of species of living corals, and the reefs are the primary habitat for literally thousands of fish species and other marine organisms (Austin 2003: 75). The reefs build up from thousands of tiny coral polyps, small carnivorous organisms that feed on small particles floating in the water. Through symbiosis with unicellular algae, these reef-building corals are the source of primary production in reef ecosystems. As they grow and mature, the polyps lay down skeletal structures of calcium carbonate upon successive generations of polyps.

Courtesy of James F. Eder

FIGURE 2.5 Mangrove forest at Darapiton River, Port Barton

Though the polyps are the chief architects of coral reefs, tube worms, mollusks, and other organisms also donate their hard skeletons. Wave action on parts of the reefs fronting the ocean and coralline algae contribute to reef-building by depositing limestone in sheets over the surface of the reef, thereby strengthening its structural integrity. Because they harbor rich marine life, coral reefs are a favored fishing destination throughout the Philippines. Palawan is home to more than half of the nation's reefs.

Palawan is also home to almost two-thirds of the nation's remaining old-growth mangrove forests. Mangroves are woody, salt-tolerant shrubs and trees located along sheltered intertidal coastlines, estuaries and lagoons. Mangroves help protect coral reefs from erosion and siltation caused by upland runoff, and they protect the coastal plain from storm winds and ocean tides. Mangroves provide vital habitat for shrimp, the locally prized and commercially valuable mud crab (*alimango*), and the juvenile stages of some species of fish (Austin 2003: 76). The mangroves most commonly found in Palawan are of the genus *Rhizophora*, made distinctive by elongated seeds that germinate and grow on the parent tree before dropping off and becoming stuck in the mud at low tide. Mangrove trees in this genus differ from those in other genera by their numerous aerial roots that form an almost impenetrable barrier to human intrusion (Figure 2.5). The roots grow upward above the mud where they become inundated at high tide and absorb oxygen from the air at low tide (Novellino 2000).

Sea grasses are flowering plants that grow underwater, attached to sandy or rocky ocean bottoms by rhizomes and roots. They prefer shallow, well-lit water in bays, inlets, and estuaries. The leaves are long and strap-shaped. Individual plants cluster together to form dense meadows that resemble terrestrial grasslands. Sea grasses have important ecological functions. One such function is to interact with coral reefs and mangroves to reduce wave energy and regulate water flow. Because of the thickness of their underground root systems, they help retain and bind sediment and serve as a buffer against storm surges. Like mangroves, sea grasses provide food and nutrients essential to the coastal environment and its marine inhabitants. Detritus formed in sea grass beds enters other food chains, and the grasses themselves constitute the staple diet of manatees and sea turtles and are a source of nourishment for fish. Sea grasses provide nursery grounds for many kinds of fish, and they are home to crabs, prawns, worms, algae, sponges, and other invertebrates. Many commercially important fish species spend part of their life cycle in sea grass beds.

In 1996, a team of researchers from Silliman University in the central Philippines counted 22 species of mangroves, eight species of sea grasses, 103 species of coral and 117 species of fish in San Vicente (San Vicente 2001; see Appendix A). Later chapters will provide greater detail about the impacts of human activities on these resources and ecosystems in San Vicente; here I will make two general points. First, an estimated 50 to 60 percent of all Filipinos live in the coastal zone. Their livelihoods are directly affected by damage to coral reefs, mangroves, and sea grass beds, even as their own efforts to secure those livelihoods are themselves sometimes one cause of that damage (Austin 2003: 77–78).

Second, a wide variety of human activities, and not just fishing, directly affect the health of coastal ecosystems. Commercial logging, shifting cultivation (described later in this chapter), and mining operations on forested hillsides all cause erosion and siltation that damage coral reefs. Cutting of mangroves for charcoal manufacture or for commercial fishpond development reduces the nutrients needed by spawning aquatic life and the nursery grounds available for marine organisms (Austin 2003: 78–81). Loss of light caused by increased sediment in bays and inlets and algae growth due to increased organic pollution both negatively impact sea grass beds. Figure 2.6, drawn from a "primer" on coastal resource issues worldwide, illustrates how these and other human activities negatively affect the well-being of coastal ecosystems and reduce the productivity of fisheries.

Terrestrial Habitats and Resources

My view of the coastal zone is broader than most. The "coastal zone" notion commonly refers to the three interlinked ecosystems just discussed—coral reefs, mangroves, and sea grass beds—and to the human-occupied strip of land immediately adjacent to the ocean. In my view, coastal zones also include the resources of coastal plains and adjacent foothills and mountainsides because these resources are important in the daily economic lives of farmers and other coastal zone residents, including those who at first glance appear to be just "fishing people."

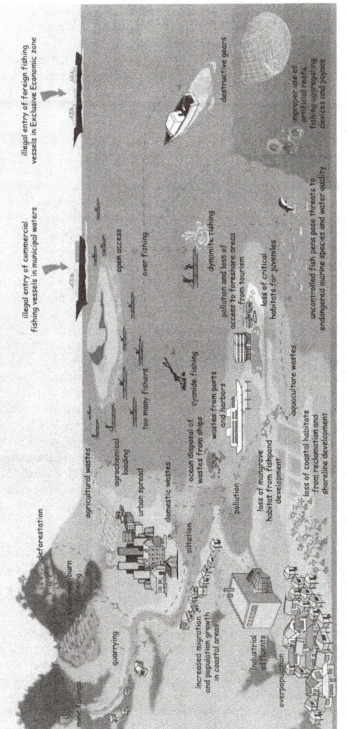

FIGURE 2.6 Human activities in the coastal zone

A local distinction, common throughout Southeast Asia, between the "interior" (*sugod*) and the "coast" (*baybay*) is helpful for envisioning terrestrial habitats and resources in San Vicente. The former is hilly or mountainous and the latter mostly flat. Underlying the interior and coastal regions of San Vicente are two common Palawan soil types, Babuyan silty clay loam and Coron clay loam (Barrera 1960). Silty clay loam is the principle soil of the coastal plain. It is friable, loose, and easy to plow. Because (unlike soils elsewhere in Palawan) it lacks subsurface stones and boulders, it affords good penetration of roots to lower layers. However, silty clay loam is so fine and sticky when wet that drainage is sometimes poor, and during the rainy season some areas become water-logged. Coron clay loam is a soil of the interior, strewn with rocks and rock fragments but reasonably fertile and extremely well drained. Its dryness and shallow structure make it even more susceptible than most soils of the sloping uplands to erosion. In some parts of the interior underlaid by Coron clay loam, the bedrock is exposed, erosion "pavements" have formed, and fragments of rock litter the ground (Barrera 1960: 54–63).

In the hilly and mountainous interior of San Vicente, four kinds of vegetative cover are common: primary forest, secondary forest (long fallow second growth), brush land (short fallow second growth), and grassland. Primary forest, rich in species diversity, is the terrestrial counterpart of the coral reef because it is the habitat for a wide variety of plants and animals, including the tropical hardwoods prized by the commercial logging industry and home builders. From the primary forest also come a variety of non-timber forest products, which local residents exploit for subsistence or for sale in local or global markets. These products include wild pigs, wild honey, orchids, rattans, and Manila copal, a tree resin. Rattans collected in San Vicente are mostly of the genus *Calamus*. Housing construction and furniture manufacture are the main uses of rattan. Some rattan furniture is sold in Puerto Princesa City, but most of the higher-quality rattan collected in San Vicente goes to factories in Manila and other cities where workers make furniture for export. Manila copal is the resinous exude of the giant *almaciga* tree, *Agathis philippensis,* one of the few species of conifers that grows in the humid tropics. *Almaciga* trees may reach 60 meters in height and have trunks 3 meters wide; the valuable resin is an ingredient in the manufacture of varnish and linoleum.

Commercial logging is now banned in Palawan, but some San Vicente residents use chain saws and *carabaw* (water buffalos) to illegally cut and haul logs to supply local furniture-making and home-construction needs. I spoke with a number of such "illegal loggers" who defended their activities by citing their own need for income and the needs of their neighbors for construction materials. They also argued that any environmental damage they caused was inconsequential, because they were only removing a few logs at a time from a very large forest. Their rationalization does not match the reality that the activities of many small-scale loggers throughout Palawan are slowly degrading the quality of the remaining primary forest, especially in areas near human settlements.

Another significant human impact on forest biodiversity stems from non-timber forest product collection and sale. Rattan extraction from the forest is faster than the rattan-bearing palms can regenerate. Injurious tapping practices and too-frequent collection of Manila copal have lead to fungus infections and widespread mortality among almaciga trees. Such pressures on non-timber forest products ultimately reflect the lack of alternative economic opportunities among people who collect and sell them, in particular the Tagbanua and other indigenous groups (see later in this chapter).

Both illegal logging and overexploitation of non-timber forest products pose resource management challenges that in important ways resemble the challenges of protecting coral reefs and other coastal resources from further degradation. Small-scale logging is easy to conceal, and it is facilitated with the connivance of sympathetic local officials who, perhaps in exchange for free wood, agree to look the other way. Exploitation of non-timber forest products is difficult to monitor, and the thresholds beyond which extraction becomes unsustainable are difficult to measure.

During the past 20 years, Palawan has received millions of dollars from international sources to fund forest conservation projects, some aimed at conservation of non-timber forest products in particular and others at forest conservation in general. One such project, the European Union–funded Palawan Tropical Forest Protection Programme (PTFPP), sought to facilitate preservation of Palawan's natural environment by implementing an integrated management approach to maintaining a series of catchments in different municipalities. Catchments are composed of interrelated ecosystems, from river headwaters and forested uplands to adjacent lowlands and coastal zones; a disturbance in one can affect another. For example, deforestation in the uplands can cause flooding on the coastal plain and siltation of coral reefs in adjacent bays. The various ecosystems that constitute a catchment are interdependent in the same way as mangrove, sea grass, and coral reefs ecosystems and they call for similarly holistic management strategies. In San Vicente, the PTFPP focused its efforts on the Inagdeng catchment, which centers on the Inagdeng River and the community of New Agutaya. These efforts included the establishment of no-entry forest reserves and the distribution of free fruit tree seedlings to upland farmers.

Secondary forest, brush land, and grassland reflect still greater degrees of human disturbance. They represent the different kinds and stages of vegetative re-growth that follow human entry into primary forest either for commercial logging or for agricultural use and human settlement. The principal agricultural use responsible for vegetative disturbance in San Vicente's forests is shifting cultivation, sometimes referred to as "slash-and-burn" agriculture and known locally as *kaingin* agriculture. Shifting cultivators use machetes and axes to clear vegetation from an area to be planted. Farmers allow the vegetation to dry and then burn it so that the ash will help to fertilize their crops. Shifting cultivators plant rice, corn, sweet potato, and cassava and can only use a particular field for one or two growing seasons before the soil is exhausted. They leave the used-up fields fallow for several years allowing them to regenerate. The length of the fallow period influences the amount and kind of vegetative re-growth. Meanwhile, shifting cultivators clear new fields elsewhere. General terms such as "second growth" and "re-growth" mask considerable variability in biodiversity and in desirability for further human use. Some once-forested land degraded by past human uses re-grows only a tough grass, *Imperata cylindrica*. Known locally as *cogon,* this grass appears on degraded soils throughout Southeast Asia. Farmers must plow it under before further cultivation is possible.

Shifting cultivation is one component of a suite of rain-fed agricultural activities on sloping lands in previously forested areas that I refer to as upland farming. Upland farmers typically employ shifting cultivation to clear forest or other vegetation from their homesteads, but over time many plant bananas, coconut palms, and fruit trees and establish permanent farms and homes. A contrasting type of agriculture I refer to as lowland farming predominates on the coastal plain. Irrigated rice fields, some recently constructed and some decades old are the most visible component of this type of farming, but lowland farmers plant vegetables and tree crops as well as rice.

ANTHROPOLOGICAL FIELDWORK
IN SAN VICENTE

Despite San Vicente's considerable appeal as a destination, I felt trepidation about it as a research site. Accustomed to working in local communities or small tribal settlements, I took seriously the established anthropological wisdom about the importance of knowing the people whose lives one proposes to study. How could I possibly come to "know" twenty thousand people in San Vicente? I dealt with this concern in several ways. First, I tried to understand municipal governance in San Vicente, both because of its formal administrative role in the lives of local residents and more specifically because it was in partnership with the municipal government that the Coastal Resource Management Project (CRMP) implemented its program.

The Municipal Government

As a lower-level political unit of the national government, the municipality of San Vicente has a mayor, a municipal council, and a variety of other elected and appointed officials. All hold office in an impressive-looking town hall overlooking the ocean. Mayors in the Philippines are administratively and politically more powerful than their counterparts in the United States, and San Vicente's mayor was a hard-charging and immensely busy individual whose political ambitions and development plans for his municipality often took him to Puerto Princesa City or to Manila. As a visiting social scientist of marginal interest, I only met him twice, in the course of two brief "courtesy calls" to announce my presence and my scholarly intentions. However, I regularly visited the Municipal Development Planning Office, where the staff always warmly and helpfully received me. Although they were not particularly familiar with anthropology, they were used to dealing with visiting researchers and generously shared current information about development problems and plans.

I should add here that I am still struck by the ease with which I, as an anthropologist and an outsider, entered any municipal hall in the Philippines, asked to speak to the Municipal Development Officer (the MDO, or an official with a similar title), who received me graciously because I was studying development in the Philippines and wanted to know what was going on locally. For example, early one morning a messenger from the municipal hall came to the lodging house where I stayed to let me know that the head official I had unsuccessfully sought out the previous afternoon was now "in," and would welcome me back at my earliest convenience! Finding people to interview during fieldwork is often difficult, but at least in the Philippines I have received unexpected and very kind assistance from local officials and community residents.

From my visits with municipal officials in San Vicente, I learned about how resource management officials viewed their roles and responsibilities regarding the CRMP. I also came to appreciate how local politics influenced resource management policies designed at the provincial and national levels, how they were implemented at the local level, and how numerous demands on the scarce financial and personnel resources of the municipal government limited the effectiveness of its resource management efforts. This information was valuable to my research, but I had still to learn about the local communities whose residents used coastal resources on a day-to-day basis and where degradation of those resources most directly affected people's lives. My second fieldwork task was to get to know these communities.

Local Communities

Table 2.1 shows the names and populations of the ten different communities that compose the municipality of San Vicente (Figure 2.3). Each is officially a *barangay,* the lowest-level governmental unit in the Philippine political system. *Barangays* in San Vicente range in population from about 700 persons to more than 4,000 persons. Each *barangay* is headed by a *kapitan,* or captain, and a six-member *barangay* council, all elected by local residents. *Barangay* officials receive only a modest government stipend in return for their service, and most work full time at other occupations.

When I began my research I knew that it would not be possible to study all ten communities equally. Limitations on my time and similarities between certain communities meant that I should specialize, but I also needed to find out basic information about each community, if only to have a means for deciding which communities to select for more careful study. Early in my research I made brief preliminary visits to each one. Upon first arriving in each community, I paid a "courtesy visit" (as such visits are known locally) to the *barangay* captain, to introduce myself and to explain the purposes of my research. If the *barangay* captain was not home, I instead sought out a member of the *barangay* council. Most *barangay* officials in San Vicente are farmers or fishermen. I had variable success in my efforts to meet them during my research, but some proved immensely helpful. Local officials were knowledgeable about local history, and they knew local residents well and could steer me toward those who could best speak about particular topics. If I was overtaken unexpectedly by nightfall or lack

T A B L E 2.1 Population of San Vicente

Community	Number of persons	Number of households
Alimanguan	2848	542
Binga	1372	254
Caruray	3526	672
New Agutaya	2111	420
New Canipo	1059	200
New Villafria	701	132
Port Barton	4140	814
Poblacion	3921	758
San Isidro	1025	213
Santo Niño	951	169
TOTAL:	**21654**	**4174**

of transportation in a remote community, I could usually count on spending the night at the house of a *barangay* official.

From my interviews with officials and other local residents during this initial round of "get acquainted" visits, I learned about how people in different communities made their livings and about their problems and concerns. I found important similarities between all ten communities. For example, in each community, some people were engaged in fishing and others in farming. I also found that communities differed significantly, and I focused my questioning on these differences. In some communities, fishing was more important; in others, farming. Local ecologies and population densities varied as well, and not all communities faced the same set of resource management problems or were equally accessible by land or by sea. Also, some communities had longer histories or a different mix of geographical and ethnic origins. Some San Vicente residents originated elsewhere on Palawan Island, in places like Taytay and Roxas (Figure 2.1), but many arrived from more distant places throughout the Philippines. Figure 2.7 shows some of the many islands in the Philippine archipelago to which the present inhabitants trace their roots.

The information I gathered about the ten communities is in Table 2.1. Poblacion, Alimanguan, and Port Barton are the most developed commercially, and each serves as a local hub for commerce with adjacent, smaller communities. Poblacion is the seat of the municipal government and lies at the end of the main highway from Roxas on the east coast of Palawan. A long, but rickety pier and a small gravel airstrip also help meet Poblacion's transportation needs. This community has a high school, a health clinic, a public market, a gas station, a lodging house, and various retail shops. Along one stretch of the bay lies the community of Panindigan, a neighborhood (*sitio*) of Poblacion consisting of more than two hundred fishing households. Panindigan also serves as a center for San Vicente's live fish trade and seaweed trade.

FIGURE 2.7 Places of origin of San Vicente residents (map)

Alimanguan rivals Poblacion for commercial leadership in San Vicente and has many of the same kinds of businesses and facilities. The same highway that ends in Poblacion also serves Alimanguan, and like Poblacion, Alimanguan has a vibrant fishing economy and is a hub for water transport to other communities and to small offshore islands. Alimanguan differs from Poblacion because it lies on a relatively broad section of the coastal plain suitable for irrigated rice farming. Agriculture in general is an important livelihood in the community. Port Barton was once the base of a large logging operation and is today home to about ten small beach resorts. These resorts serve domestic and international tourists drawn to explore the beaches, coral reefs, and small islands lying offshore. Passenger jeeps originating in Puerto Princesa City travel to and from Port Barton daily along a rough gravel road, carrying both local residents and resort-bound tourists.

Caruray, the largest and southernmost community, is similar to the first three communities in population size. Both fishing and farming are important in Caruray, but the community lacks roads connecting it with Poblacion and other points in San Vicente, and it is primarily oriented toward Puerto Princesa City. A silica mine operates in Caruray, and small-scale gold miners sometimes try their luck panning in a local river. Many indigenous Tagbanua live in Caruray and collect rattan, honey, and tree resin in the heavily forested interior. Popular home industries include charcoal-making and shingle-making, the latter manufactured with the fronds of the *nipa* palm, which grows along rivers and estuaries.

San Vicente's remaining six communities are for the most part smaller and decidedly rural. Binga, the northernmost community, resembles Caruray in the south in that it is not connected by a road to the rest of San Vicente. It takes 1 to 2 hours by boat to reach Binga from Alimanguan or Poblacion, and many Binga residents find it easier to trade with and to send their children to high school in the larger and more commercially developed communities around Malampaya Sound in the northern municipality of Taytay, to which a road has recently opened. Also like Caruray, Binga's population includes relatively large numbers of indigenous Tagbanua engaged in the collection and sale of forest products.

New Canipo is a 45-minute boat ride from Alimanguan. Like Binga, it is only reached by the sea, but a road now under construction will link it with the highway in Alimanguan. Most New Canipo residents are from the island of Cuyo, an island that is part of Palawan Province and lies midway between Palawan Island and the Visayan Islands in the Sulu Sea (Figure 2.7). Upland farming supplemented by subsistence fishing is the predominant economic activity. Santo Niño, lying just north of Alimanguan, is populated largely by fishing people from Samar Island and elsewhere in the Visayan Islands (Figure 2.7). In the past, many residents of Santo Niño were heavily involved in compressor-aided fishing, a now-prohibited practice associated with cyanide use and coral reef destruction. I might have selected Santo Niño for further study, but people there were reportedly angry over the prohibition of compressor use, and I feared that they might resist my efforts to study resource management issues there.

San Isidro, New Agutaya, and New Villafria are primarily farming communities. The first two are composed largely of migrants and their offspring from Agutaya, another island of the Palawan region that lies near Cuyo in the Sulu Sea. New Villafria is composed primarily of indigenous Tagbanua and migrants from Cuyo and their offspring.

Based on my preliminary round of visits to these ten communities and on subsequent advice from municipal government officials, I selected four communities for further study: Poblacion, New Agutaya, Alimanguan, and New Canipo (see Table 2.1). In Poblacion, I was attracted to the bustling fishing district of Panindigan and its various marine products enterprises. Because its residents originate from all over the Philippines, Panindigan appeared a convenient microcosm of San Vicente. Hereafter, I refer to Panindigan as one of my four study "communities," but technically, it is only a district or neighborhood of Poblacion and does not have the same political status as the other three communities, all of which, like Poblacion, are *barangays*.

New Agutaya interested me because farming was the most important liveli-hood and because some residents were involved in beach seining, a controversial and nominally prohibited fishing activity. I had participated in beach seining on the first day of my fieldwork in San Vicente, already described in Chapter 1. Composed largely of Visayan-speaking peoples, Alimanguan was attractive for study because of the prominence of both fishing and farming in community economic life. In many Alimanguan households people engaged in both fishing and farming at various times during the year. The community seemed an ideal place to explore my ideas about how both fishing and farming peoples co-depend on the same coastal zone resources.

New Canipo was almost entirely a farming community, but some residents engaged on small-scale subsistence fishing from outrigger canoes. This community stood at the opposite end of a continuum from the commercially oriented com-munity of Panindigan, where fishing is the only economic activity in most house-holds. I might have chosen San Isidro or New Villafria for the same reason, but they (like the other three communities in my set of four) had road transportation, and I wanted to include a community like New Canipo that was reachable only by boat. I also chose New Canipo for sentimental reasons. I have traveled several times to Cuyo and I conducted long-term fieldwork in San Jose, a Cuyonon farming community near Puerto Princesa City. I learned to speak Cuyonon fluently and came to enjoy interacting with Cuyonon over a shared set of cultural under-standings. I no longer do fieldwork in San Jose, but I continue to visit close friends there regularly. Several of them suggested that I visit cousins and other relatives in New Canipo, whom I later looked up, much to their surprise.

Studying People

Having selected these four communities, I turned to my third and most impor-tant fieldwork task: studying the lives of the people who lived in them. This task lay at the heart of my research, and here I followed several lines of approach. For two of the communities, Panindigan (where fishing predominated) and New Agutaya (where farming predominated), I designed a brief household survey and employed a local female research assistant to help me collect the survey data. The survey included questions about the ages, educational attainments, geographical origins, and occupations of household members; about ownership of farmland, fishing boats and equipment, and other productive assets; and about religious affiliation and the language spoken at home. We eventually completed 40 surveys in each community, representing about 10 percent of the total number of households in New Agutaya and about 20 percent in Panindigan. I devoted proportionately more attention to Panindigan than to New Agutaya with my survey research because Panindigan was more ethnically complex than New Agutaya and because of my particular interest in fishing.

The households included in these surveys were representative of their communities; I did not choose them randomly. Before deciding which households in each community would be included in the survey, my research assistant and I sat down with the *barangay* captain and several local community leaders to seek approval for the survey and their advice on how best to proceed. I wanted the survey to adequately consider differences between households in economic well-being and social status. In each community, we asked several knowledgeable local residents to divide local households into three groups, representing high, medium, and low socioeconomic status. Still working together, we then selected twelve to fifteen households that they considered to be representative of occupations and modes of resource use at each status level. Then they indicated which members of these households would most likely be willing to participate in the survey. Most of the individuals we selected proved to be willing survey respondents, but a few were difficult to contact or, for various reasons, were unwilling to participate, and we later replaced them with respondents from similar households.

Information from these surveys helps illustrate the diversity of geographical backgrounds and ethnic groups found in these two communities and, by extension, in San Vicente as a whole. Table 2.2 shows the places of birth of household co-heads and languages spoken at home in the forty Panindigan households and forty New Agutaya households included in the survey. Most households in San Vicente and elsewhere in the Philippines are co-headed by a man and woman who are also husband and wife. Some households have only one head, because of the separation or death of a spouse. Most places of birth shown in Table 2.2 are islands. Some of these islands, like Cebu, are themselves also provinces; other islands, like Cuyo, are parts of larger provinces. Other places of birth are cities such as Manila or provinces on very large islands, such as Ilocos on Luzon or Zamboanga on Mindanao. Table 2.2 shows that even in this relatively small sample of households in two communities, a remarkable diversity of geographical origins is present, especially in the case of Panindigan origins that lie in the central Visayan Islands region of the Philippines. Based on this sample, the islands of Masbate, Samar, Negros, and Agutaya have been particularly important "donors" to the present population of San Vicente.

Table 2.2 also shows languages associated with the places of origin and which ones are spoken in the sample households. Some associations between languages and geographical areas are clear from their names. For example, Cebuano is the language in Cebu, Masbateño is the language in Masbate, and Agutaynen is the language in Agutaya. The names of other languages do not sound like the home islands of their speakers. For example, Waray is the language of migrants from Samar and Leyte, and Ilonggo is the language of migrants from portions of Panay and Negros. Many San Vicente residents speak two or more languages, one of which is typically Tagalog, the national language

T A B L E 2.2 **Places of Birth and Languages in the Home in Panindigan and New Agutaya**

	Panindigan	New Agutaya
Place of Birth:		
Agutaya	2	38
Albay	2	
Cebu	3	
Cuyo	6	2
Ilocos		2
Leyte	4	
Manila	1	
Masbate	17	
Mindoro		2
Negros	2	18
Palawan	16	15
Panay	2	
Romblon	3	
Samar	12	
Sorsogon	4	
Zamboanga	1	
Total:	**75**	**77**
Language in Home:		
Agutaynen		22
Cebuano	5	
Cuyonon	4	
Ilonggo	2	11
Masbateño	4	
Tagalog	22	7
Waray	3	
Total:	**40**	**40**

and an important lingua franca in Palawan. Tagalog is spoken throughout the Philippines, and it is the native language of about 35 to 40 percent of all Filipinos, particularly those who inhabit the greater Manila area and provinces in central and southern Luzon.

"Language in the home" in Table 2.2 refers to the language that adult members of the household use to speak to each other and to their children. In preparing this table, I selected the one language that appeared most important in each household, but in some households two languages were used, one between the adult co-heads and the other (usually Tagalog) with the children. In other households, the co-heads each spoke a different language and used Tagalog to talk to each other. Relatively few native speakers of Tagalog have settled in San Vicente and where Tagalog appears as the main language in the home, it is usually because parents who speak another language are speaking Tagalog with their children to better prepare them for elementary school, where Tagalog and English are the mediums of instruction.

While my research assistant was administering the household surveys in two of the communities, I was busy in all four communities conducting participant observation and informal interviewing. In fishing households, I asked about crew composition, about how fishermen selected their fishing grounds, and about how they marketed fish. I asked about nets, baits, lures, and other fishing techniques, and I asked about how individual fishermen experienced coastal resource depletion and how they felt about efforts to curtail or prohibit destructive fishing practices that might cause such depletion. In farming house-holds, I asked about cropping practices, the availability and reliability of irriga-tion water, and seasonal uses of household and hired labor. In both kinds of households, I paid particular attention to the role of women in day-to-day and longer-term economic affairs.

As I interviewed residents in these four communities about their daily lives, I discovered that some also belonged to other kinds of social groupings that later proved important to my research. Each community had a women's association and several church congregations. In Alimanguan and Panindigan, opportunities to obtain small loans from microfinance organizations had stimulated the forma-tion of several borrower's associations. Still other associations, including those of fishing boat owners and beach resort operators, crosscut local community bound-aries. Some of these associations were inactive or existed only on paper, but I followed up on each one, hoping to turn up helpful leads.

I met weekly with my research assistant to discuss progress with the household surveys and to compare notes on our respective findings. The survey information sometimes suggested new lines of questioning, as when husbands and wives reported belonging to different religions, a surprising circumstance by American standards, or when they used two different languages at home. Sometimes I asked my research assistant to follow up and seek clarification about particular responses, especially if they appeared sensitive or involved women. Often I asked follow-up questions myself, to expand my opportunities to meet more people and to thank them for their help with my research.

During my fieldwork, I stayed in lodging houses or with families in Pobla-cion, Alimanguan, or New Canipo. From those places, I could reach on foot most of the people whom I wished to interview. From these communities, I also made day-long forays by boat to other locales, and on occasion I stayed overnight in a distant community or on an offshore island by prior arrangement with a family I had already met, or one suggested by a relative. From experience, I learned which people were best to ask about fishing or fish marketing, or with whom to practice my Cebuano or learn local history. In the early morning or late afternoon, the beach was a good place to meet people. I never did meet, or much

Courtesy of James F. Eder

FIGURE 2.8 Houses of fishing families at Alimanguan

less come to know, all twenty thousand of San Vicente's residents, but I did eventually meet and talk with a good number of them, from all walks of local life (see Figure 2.8).

A BRIEF HISTORY OF SAN VICENTE

On an island that itself has long been celebrated as the nation's "last frontier," San Vicente was one of the last places in the Philippines to be settled. Its municipal government was created as late as 1972 by combining ten communities previously included in the older municipalities of Taytay and Puerto Princesa. Remote and inaccessible, and reachable only by boat or on foot, these communities were then populated by approximately 6,000 hardy settlers who had been attracted by San Vicente's virgin forest soils and rich fishing grounds.

Farmland and fishing grounds did not put San Vicente on the national map. After all, these could be found elsewhere in the frontier Philippines. Rather, in 1981, then-president Ferdinand Marcos granted one of the largest logging concessions in Palawan's history to a wealthy timber baron who had grown rich exporting timber from Indonesia in the 1970s. The concession was located in the lush tropical hardwood forests behind Port Barton, in the southern part of the municipality (Figure 2.3). In a few short years after beginning operations, Pagdanan Timber Products became the largest employer in the municipality. To support its operations, the company constructed a sawmill, a pier, and a road connecting Port Barton with the national highway on the east side of Palawan. In the years that followed and as logging operations continued, San Vicente's population swelled with new migrants, many seeking employment in the logging industry.

Pagdanan Timber Products and its voracious appetite for logs eventually galvanized the environmental movement in Palawan and became a lightening rod for criticism about how government officials had mismanaged the island's natural resources. In a lengthy and acrimonious political battle, local environmental activists became the targets of intimidation and physical threats, and the company's owner vowed to cut "every last tree" to which he was entitled. In the end, the government cancelled the controversial logging permit. Succumbing to pressure from local and international environmentalists, in 1992 the provincial government of Palawan declared a total logging ban to preserve the island's remaining stands of primary forest. When logging operations ceased, some former employees drifted away but many remained in San Vicente and turned to farming or fishing. A variety of agricultural products from San Vicente reach external markets, but the municipality's most visible market links today concern fishing. Fresh fish of all kinds goes by truck daily to the east coast of Palawan for sale in Puerto Princesa City and for transshipment to Manila. Several times weekly, a small plane arrives to transport live fish bound for restaurants in Hong Kong and Taiwan. Special arrangements govern the marketing of squid and seaweed, farmed by fishing households seeking an alternative livelihood in the face of coastal resource depletion.

OTHER HISTORIES

I am confident that most San Vicente residents would recognize this brief, "official" account of their municipality's history as essentially correct, although it is not the history that any resident would likely have spoken or written. I learned about the existence of numerous local histories involving the municipality's constituent communities, most of which are older than San Vicente itself. Even the names of these communities reveal different orientations to local history. Port Barton was named for an Englishman who surveyed the region in the 1940s. New Agutaya, New Canipo, and New Villafria were all named to commemorate the geographical origins of their migrant founding residents, similar to New Hampshire and New Bedford in the United States. San Isidro and Santo Niño commemorate Catholic religious traditions and are named for the patron saints of those two communities. Alimanguan is named for the abundance of crabs that early settlers encountered on its shores, and Poblacion acquired its name as the seat of the municipal government. Two communities, Binga and Caruray, still bear their aboriginal Tagbanua names. Binga is named for a particular species of shell, thousands of which people say washed up on its shore decades ago following a typhoon in the Calamiane

Island region of northern Palawan. Caruray's name derives from the Tagbanua word *maruway,* which means "easy going" or "easy life."

The varied names of local communities signal the considerable differences between San Vicente's inhabitants in ethnic background and geographical origin. In Panindigan, an often-heard anecdote is that by walking along the beach from one group of houses to the next, one passes from Bicol, to Masbate, to Samar, and then on to Cuyo, all points near and far in the Philippine archipelago from which its inhabitants have migrated. As an anthropologist, I knew that the cultural differences associated with such diverse origins would provide an important window into the structure of local economic and social life.

Ethnic diversity in the Philippines revolves around distinctions between Christian Filipinos, Muslim Filipinos, and indigenous Filipinos. Christian Filipinos are sometimes called "lowland" Filipinos because of their association with the nation's long-settled plains and river valleys. Some scholars also call them "Hispanized Filipinos" to emphasize the formative role of the Spanish colonial period, which saw the introduction of Catholicism and other Spanish influences on Philippine culture and society. In the southern Philippines, many inhabitants were Islamized rather than Hispanized. Ethnically distinct groups of Muslim Filipinos, also called "Philippine Muslims," today reside there. Widely scattered groups of indigenous peoples inhabiting the mountains and hinterland regions of the nation mostly isolated from Spanish or Muslim contact retain much of their traditional cultural practices. Christian Filipinos account for more than 80 percent of the nation's total population; Muslim Filipinos and indigenous Filipinos each account for about 10 percent.

The Cuyonon, Agutaynen, and Visayan migrants who settled in San Vicente all fall into this first broad category of Christian Filipinos. No Muslim Filipinos presently reside in San Vicente, but Muslim traders occasionally visited the area in years past. Most Muslims in Palawan live in the south, but some have moved northward to Puerto Princesa City and beyond. Three peoples are indigenous to Palawan Island: the Batak, who inhabit the forested mountains of the northeastern part of the island; the Pala'wan, who inhabit the foothills and the mountains of the south; and the Tagbanua, who inhabit the central and northern parts of the island, including in San Vicente.

San Vicente residents arrived from different places and at different times, some before 1972 but most after. The different geographical and cultural origins and times of arrival of San Vicente's residents have colored their perspectives on the past and the present. To understand how these residents might cooperate in the management of their coastal resources, we need to investigate the meanings and values they attach to these resources. Next I consider how San Vicente's history might look from the perspectives of indigenous Tagbanua residents, early Cuyonon migrants, and more recent Visayan migrants.

Tagbanua

Tagbanua in San Vicente are concentrated in the communities of Binga, Caruray, and New Villafria. They identify locally as *Tandolanen* Tagbanua and are linguistically and culturally distinct from the other groups of Tagbanua who reside elsewhere on Palawan. Tagbanua in San Vicente have long intermarried with Cuyonon and other peoples of migrant origin. Gradually Tagbanua have ceased to practice many of their own cultural traditions, and their everyday lives today are very much like those of their non-indigenous neighbors, although in general they are less well off economically. Some Tagbanua were surprised that I knew of and had even attended Tagbanua *pagdiwata* ceremonies held elsewhere in Palawan. These intriguing ceremonies, of a type once common among indigenous peoples throughout island Southeast Asia, occurred in the postharvest period and combined shamanistic curing, consumption of large quantities of "rice wine" (technically, rice beer), and ritual thanks to the ancestral spirits for a bountiful rice harvest (Fox 1982). Postharvest ceremonies have long since disappeared in the San Vicente area and only the oldest Tagbanua residents remembered attending one.

Land alienation and displacement from the coastal zone by Christian Filipino settlers, along with the erosion of cultural traditions, figure prominently in the narratives of older Tagbanua residents regarding the history of San Vicente. They remember a time when Tagbanua settlements were located along the beach front and only a few non-Tagbanua lived there or even visited the area. "We all fished then, but now, no more," said one older man, referring to a time when Tagbanua regularly fished from the beach and farmed on the coastal plain. The history of Tagbanua in San Vicente parallels that of indigenous peoples throughout Palawan. The settlement of the island by migrants from elsewhere in the Philippines began in earnest in the years following World War II. Displaced from the coastal plain and pushed into the interior of the island by successive waves of settlers, indigenous peoples were marginalized economically and socially. The Philippine government regarded them as squatters on public land that was better opened to more productive uses. Many, including those who live in San Vicente, are enmeshed in debilitating creditor-debtor relationships with their settler neighbors. Tagbanua and other indigenous peoples on Palawan remain culturally distinct, but as they have been incorporated into the Philippine state, they have come to occupy the subordinate bottom rung of a wider class system. Their position in Philippine society is comparable with that of many Native Americans in the United States (Eder 1987).

In recent decades, the circumstances of indigenous people in Palawan have changed for the better. Inspired and funded by international environmentalist organizations such as the World Wildlife Fund and Conservation International, several nongovernmental organizations (NGOs) based in Puerto Princesa City today work with indigenous peoples in Palawan to protect portions of their remaining ancestral lands from further encroachment and resource exploitation. These NGOs draw support from recent government legislation promising indigenous people security of tenure on a specified portion of their ancestral domain in return for a promise (embodied in a written resource management plan) to manage the resources within that domain on a sustainable basis. Several such programs involve the ancestral coastal lands and resources of Tagbanua elsewhere in Palawan. For the most part, these programs target still-forested lands to manage them on a more sustainable basis to support the collection and sale of rattan and other non-timber forest products upon which many Tagbanua today depend for their livelihoods. One NGO in Puerto Princesa City is presently helping the Tagbanua in Alimanguan to protect one thousand hectares of nearby forest land under this program. In addition, the same NGO recently helped Alimanguan Tagbanua to construct a small local domestic water system to serve the neighborhood where many of them reside.

Tagbanua in San Vicente continue to identify themselves as indigenous people. As the region's original inhabitants, others refer to them (often condescendingly) as "natives" or as *naturales*. Today they mostly engage in shifting cultivation, wage labor, and the collection and sale of non-timber forest products, but not in fishing. I made several close Tagbanua friends in San Vicente. Some knew of my research with Tagbanua and other indigenous people elsewhere in Palawan, and the opportunity to speak with people who were comfortable with Cuyonon was a welcome respite from my efforts to learn Cebuano or to work in Tagalog or English. The San Vicente Tagbanua have many important and interesting stories to tell, but their contemporary lives and concerns lie mostly beyond the scope this book.

Cuyonon and Agutaynen

The second category of local residents consists of Cuyonon and Agutaynen, peoples who originated elsewhere in the Palawan region, on small islands lying between Palawan Island and Panay Island, and who characteristically combine an upland mixed farming or irrigated rice cultivation with part-time dependence on fishing. Cuyonon and Agutaynen migrants first settled in San Vicente during the 1950s and, as elsewhere on Palawan Island, they were responsible for most of the pioneer forest clearance on the coastal plain. In the process, they intermingled and intermarried with other migrants. The daily lives of Cuyonon and Agutaynen today resemble those of millions of other rural Filipinos throughout the archipelago. However, they have distinctive cultural histories related to the Spanish colonial period and, in particular, to Spain's largely fruitless effort to wrest control of the Sulu region from sea-faring Muslim peoples emanating from the southern Philippines and Borneo. As part of this effort, Spain established churches and constructed garrisoned forts on both Cuyo and Agutaya early in the seventeenth century. The oral histories of migrants from these two islands center on the rich social life that developed in otherwise isolated island communities during this period.

On Cuyo, social life centered on events associated with the Catholic religious calendar. At the annual village fiesta, everyone attended plays or parodies (*komedia*) acted out to music played on locally manufactured flutes, drums, and banjos. The most common play reenacted the violent seventeenth-century confrontations between Christians and Muslims at Cuyo. Cockfights were and remain standard fiesta fare. Cuyonon today pride themselves on their Catholicism. On their home island, they developed a particularly rich set of traditions associated with the celebration of Easter. Throughout Lent, groups of older women gathered to sing a Cuyonon translation of the Passion (*pabasa*). Villagers sat and listened for hours to their eerie falsetto voices. Holy Week involved a steady progression of masses and processions. On Saturday night, people remained awake and gathered in the plaza to listen to humorous riddle-like and innuendo-laden exchanges (*erekay*) between old men and women. Before dawn people attended mass and then joined one of two processions whose meeting would symbolize the reuniting of Mary and the resurrected Christ on Easter Sunday. The Cuyonon in San Vicente today no longer practice some of these traditions, but during Holy Week in New Canipo and New Villafria, one can still hear the singing of the Passion and participate in the Easter sunrise processions. Although these Catholic religious traditions resemble those in many other parts of the world, the distinctive aspects that Cuyonon have imparted to them are an important dimension of contemporary Cuyonon ethnic identity (Eder 1982; 2004).

The overarching theme of Tagbanua narratives about the past in San Vicente was the loss of land and other resources, and the loss of language and cultural traditions. The most prominent theme in Cuyonon narratives was the hardships of pioneer forest clearance and frontier life. Cuyonon accounts of San Vicente's history center on migration from Cuyo, at first annually, to grow upland rice in Palawan's rich primary forest soil, and then later to establish permanent settlements up and down Palawan's coasts. Cuyonon migrants established several of San Vicente's communities, including Poblacion, the municipal seat, during the 1950s and early 1960s. At that time, sailboats were still in use for inter-island travel in the Palawan region, and Cuyonon accounts of the early settlement period often mention the uncertainties and hazards of ocean voyages as well as the endemic malaria and the pain of separation from loved ones back in Cuyo. Cuyonon see themselves as having founded San Vicente. They emphasize that they arrived well before the Visayans. The oldest Cuyonon migrants typically began their accounts by reporting where they stood in the order of arrival of the various "founding families." "When we arrived in 1957, only ten other families were already established here" was how one such prideful narrative began. "We were among the originals here" was another expression I often heard.

Older Cuyonon migrants spoke of the abundance of marine resources they encountered upon arrival. One early migrant described an abundance of squid, "more than we could possibly eat or sell," and another said there were so many crabs in the inter-tidal zone that she only caught the largest ones and did not bother with the rest. When called upon to do so, Cuyonon settlers acknowledge the prior presence of Tagbanua in San Vicente. With a perspective reminiscent of European settlement of the Americas, early Cuyonon settlers viewed Tagbanua as "uncivilized" and as part of the natural landscape (recall the term *naturales* earlier). In their view, the social landscape was yet to be constructed.

Visayans

The third category of local inhabitants consists of migrants from still more distant locales in the Philippines, particularly "Visayans," as Cebuanos, Warays, Masbateños, and others from the central Philippines are known locally. This category also includes migrants from Mindoro, Bicol, and from Cebuano-speaking parts of

Mindanao. These migrants began settling in San Vicente during the 1960s and 1970s, and most make their living primarily by fishing. Visayans are one of the largest and most vibrant ethnic groups in the Philippines, and over time, they have expanded out of the central Philippines region to settle much of northern Mindanao and coastal Palawan. High population densities, lack of economic opportunities, and political unrest on home islands, coupled with deteriorating social relationships between the poor and their landlords and other patrons, explain this Visayan diaspora. Some migrant Visayans sought new farmland on land-rich frontiers such as Mindanao and Palawan, but many others turned to fishing.

Migrants from the eastern Visayas region, including the islands of Cebu, Bohol, Samar and Leyte, are among the foremost maritime peoples in the Philippines. Movement is a major theme in the culture of Visayan fishing people. Many move seasonally between different fishing grounds and ports of call, depending on the monsoon winds. The Philippines experiences two monsoon seasons; the northeast monsoon (*amihan*) blows from January to May, and the southeast monsoon (*habagat*) blows from June to November. How much rain each monsoon brings, and when it starts and ends, varies with location, but monsoonal storms make navigation and fishing difficult and sometimes swamp or capsize fishing boats. Fishing peoples in the region coordinate their movements with the shifting monsoon winds, seeking leeward fishing grounds and leaving windward ones. Visayan fishing peoples developed a chain of settlements in different parts of the central Philippine archipelago and established social networks in those settlements to reactivate on a seasonal basis.

Richer fishing grounds than what they knew at home figure prominently in Visayan accounts of their migration and settlement of Palawan. Just as land scarcity forced Cuyonon to leave Cuyo, depletion of traditional fishing grounds forced Visayan migrants to leave the Visayan Islands. Visayan narratives of the past emphasize mobility. Many Visayan migrants established footholds and stayed 1 or 2 years in other parts of Palawan before finally settling permanently in San Vicente. Visayan migrants typically view both Tagbanua and Cuyonon as members of a single category of sedentary and agriculturally oriented local residents who had underutilized coastal resources, either out of disinterest or technological backwardness. Visayans thus see themselves much as Cuyonon do, as having played a founding role in the development of the area's economy and society. Like Cuyonon, Visayans have appropriated and to a degree rewritten local history to emphasize their own past sacrifices, and they ignore the earlier presence of Tagbanua and Cuyonon ranking themselves first by order of arrival to help legitimize their social position relative to the other groups.

Migrant Visayan fishermen visit San Vicente waters on a seasonal basis. During my fieldwork, I visited briefly with a number of Visayan boat crews. Some had only put ashore overnight to rest and re-supply, but others stayed for several weeks at a time, fishing and visiting relatives living nearby. Migratory fishermen typically travel in groups of five or more boats. One fisherman jokingly referred to his group of more than ten boats as the "Cebuano armada." I was fascinated by the way of life of these people, but I concluded that it would be difficult to study. Local residents, including some of Visayan origin, expressed a dim view of such seemingly rootless fishing peoples. "They are like grass floating in the middle of the ocean," said one Cebuano resident of Panindigan; "they just go wherever the waves carry them." Another local resident even characterized them as "sea robbers," implying an image of strangers who turn up unexpectedly, raid the local stock of coastal resources, and then move on to another place. This resident was particularly annoyed that local residents were expected to manage coastal resources more sustainably, but migratory fishermen could still use those resources as they wished and not share in the responsibility for their proper management.

These one-dimensional, thumbnail characterizations of San Vicente's residents and their histories do not do justice to the considerable cultural similarities and differences within and between these ethnic groups. For example, some Visayans primarily farm and some Cuyonon primarily fish for a living. Class and other kinds of differences are at play as well. These brief characterizations do not tell us whether people choose to make their living in a certain way because of their ethnic background or their "culture," or because of their time of arrival or other circumstances. Some local residents argue that Visayans fish for a living because they are naturally attracted to the ocean, just as Cuyonon are attracted to land. Others point out that Cuyonon migrants arrived before others, at a time when they could more easily acquire farm land. This is a familiar dilemma in anthropological fieldwork: do cultural values or material and historical circumstances best account for the differences that we observe between different groups of people? I tend to favor the latter explanation, but for now my point is that San Vicente's coastal communities contain considerable ethnic and ecological variability, and that the nature of their dependence upon coastal resources varies widely, within and between them.

TONY'S STORY

Within each local, "cultural" history lie individual men and women, each with their own stories to tell about how they came to live in San Vicente and why they currently make their livings in different ways. The story of Tony, one of my best friends in San Vicente whom I sometimes thought of as "Tony the cool guy," nicely illustrates the varied and sometimes surprising life histories of local inhabitants (see Figure 2.9). I first met Tony after another friend pointed him out as a long-time squid fisherman. I sought him out to ask whether squid stocks had suffered the same decline as fish stocks in recent years. At first glance, Tony appeared to be just one more migrant Visayan fisherman who had left home for richer fishing grounds in Palawan. As I got to know Tony, I learned that he had never fished in his youth or before coming to Palawan. The son of a hospital attendant in a town on Samar Island, Tony had a talent for music. To support himself while a college student in Catbalogan, Samar's capital, Tony joined a band that played all around northern Samar. After enjoying a certain degree of

Courtesy of James F. Eder

FIGURE 2.9 Tony with his fishing gear

local fame, the band successfully auditioned in Manila to play for American troops then serving in Vietnam. When the band, named the "Tiptop," returned from Vietnam, they established themselves in Olongapo City and entertained American military personnel stationed at a nearby naval base. Here Tony met and married Winnie, likewise from Samar. Winnie's father had migrated to the Olongapo area to open a furniture shop that specialized in selling rattan furniture to American servicemen and women.

All this changed abruptly in 1992, with the abrogation of the U.S.–Philippines bases agreement and the withdrawal of American military forces from the Olongapo naval base and nearby Clark airfield. The local entertainment industry collapsed, and people like Tony and Winnie had to seek new livelihoods. Seeing only peasant unrest and lack of economic opportunity back in their home province of Samar, Tony and Winnie decided to migrate and start over in Palawan. They first settled farther north, in Malampaya Sound, where Winnie had a distant cousin, but in seeking greater opportunities, they soon moved to San Vicente where Tony took up squid fishing.

ISLAND DIVERSITY ON A GLOBAL STAGE

The inhabitants of San Vicente go about their everyday lives on an island of remarkable natural and cultural diversity. In the ocean, on the coastal plain, and on the forested hillsides of San Vicente are found diverse marine and terrestrial habitats. Each habitat appears distinct, but the well-being of each habitat depends in good part on the health of its ecosystemic relationships with nearby habitats. Living in this coastal zone are people of diverse geographical origins and ethnic backgrounds. Some are indigenous and some are migrants; the latter have originated from throughout the Philippines. San Vicente's inhabitants may today live side-by-side, but they exploit coastal zone resources and earn their livings in different ways, depending in part on these differences in origin and cultural background.

Tony's story illustrates the inadequacy of such general labels as "local resident" and "migrant fisherman" and suggests some of the challenges that the diverse experiences and perspectives of local residents pose for anthropological fieldwork. Tony's story also stands as a reminder that even in such seemingly distant and isolated locales as San Vicente, the lives of local residents unfold in a world of global interconnectedness, where economic and political actors and forces often lying far beyond the boundaries of local communities powerfully influence local experiences and developments.

3

✳

San Vicente in the Global Economy

C oastal resource use in San Vicente unfolds on a global stage where unseen actors and government policies written from afar powerfully influence the exploitation of local resources. The Philippine government has historically viewed natural resources as an endowment to be extracted and sold to finance its activities, including the promotion of economic growth. The Philippine state is relatively weak politically and economically, and it has traditionally allocated the rights to extract resources as a reward for political support or to attract foreign investment. I will show in this chapter that in their efforts to earn a living from coastal resources, local fishers and farmers are on an unequal footing with the politically powerful domestic and transnational elites that dominate the competition to extract and sell those resources, and those elites care little about the well-being of local residents.

THE NATURE OF PHILIPPINE DEVELOPMENT

The Philippines is rich in natural resources and human capital, yet its people are among the poorest in Southeast Asia. Versions of this harsh observation have circulated for decades among outside observers, local social scientists, and government officials and have penetrated the consciousness of millions of ordinary Filipinos. Despite the noticeable poverty, the nation has not gone without "development." The evidence of decades of development, planned and unplanned, is everywhere, from the near-universal adoption of high-yielding rice varieties and the extensive and export-oriented coconut and banana plantations in rural areas to the labor-intensive export industries, huge private and government buildings, and shopping malls of the cities. The problem has not been the absence of "development" but a particularly debilitating kind of development, one that has enriched a minority of citizens while proving inordinately destructive of the environment and of the well-being of millions of other Filipinos, about half of whom lack adequate food, shelter, and health care and who today continue to live below the government's poverty line.

How could this have happened, in a country that 50 years ago was among the most prosperous in Southeast Asia, and despite decades of large-scale, international development programs intended to improve the general welfare? Much of the answer lies in the nature of the Philippine political system and the nation's policies regarding natural resources and economic growth. The autonomy and capacity of the Philippine state to do anything, including improve the general welfare, are constrained by elite penetration of the state and the exclusionary nature of Philippine democracy. Political dynasties remain a continuing feature of Philippine politics, and personalities rather than issues define political parties. A crucial constraint is the relatively unfettered ability of the wealthy and politically powerful to get their way, including their way with the exploitation of natural resources, an ability captured by such terms as "predatory elite" and "plunder economy" (Broad and Cavanagh 1993; Hutchcroft 1998).

The wealthy have historically "gotten their way" with natural resource exploitation in the Philippines not just because of the power of wealth but because of a legal framework that views the natural environment as the source of land and raw materials needed for commodity production and economic growth. In addition, in the nation's political system, land grants, forest and mineral concessions, and other rights to extract natural resources are prime instruments for rewarding allies and engendering political patronage. Thus abetted by the apparatus of the state, domestic and transnational economic and political elites (often the same individuals) engage in a wide variety of resource extraction enterprises (particularly logging, mining, and fishing) with a minimum of government regulation and with widespread environmental devastation as one outcome. Bello (1988) characterizes the Philippine political system as a form of "institutionalized looting." The rights to exploit the nation's resources come with strings attached. The government expects the owners of resource extraction enterprises to return to the government a portion of their profits, in the form of a concessionary fee or a lease payment. Government laws and policies intended to prevent or limit the environmental damage take a back seat to profits and fees. Much of the income from resource extraction intended for government coffers disappears into the pockets of corrupt officials and politicians. Non-enforcement of penalties and other forms of government inaction have meant that environmental misbehavior in the Philippines has usually gone unpunished.

The Logging Industry

The Philippines has a vigorous tradition of investigative journalism, which means that unpunished resource abuse and government corruption do not go unnoticed. Some of the best known cases of corruption and plunder concern the commercial logging industry during its heyday from the 1960s to the early 1980s, when the Philippines became one of the top timber exporters in the world by liquidating most of its old growth and most commercially valuable forests (the Philippines is a net wood importer). Under the administration of former President Ferdinand Marcos (1965–1986), the timber license agreements issued by the government to logging concessionaires and intended as a tool of forest management and a source of revenue for government coffers were instead used by the president to enrich his friends, family members, and political supporters.

One such timber license issued to Herminio Disini, a Marcos business associate, covered a forested area of nearly 200,000 hectares in northern Luzon, in clear violation of a constitutional provision that no single individual or corporation could have license to forest concessions in excess of 100,000 hectares. Alfonso Lim, another business associate, during his tenure with several corporations, eventually presided over timber concessions in Mindanao exceeding 600,000 hectares. Others who benefited from the often frenzied distribution of timber license agreements during the Marcos years included the president's mother and brother and two of his uncles. What the president gave, he could also take away. As a reward for the millions of pesos that Felipe Ysmael Jr. allegedly contributed to President Marcos's 1965 election campaign, he later received a license for 50,000 hectares of forest land in Quirino Province, on the eastern coast of Luzon. In 1983, Marcos declared a logging ban in Quirino and cancelled Ysmael's license ostensibly in the interest of conserving the remaining forest. And yet a year later, Marcos awarded half of the former concession to an official in his administration and the other half to his sister, both of whom were in the logging business (Vitug 1993: 13–22). His opponents believe that President Marcos received hundreds of millions of dollars in kickbacks from his various timber license-granting schemes. After the fall of Marcos, the new government of President Corazon Aquino took over many of the companies set up to profit from plunder and began efforts to recover some of the ill-gotten wealth and lost government revenue of the Marcos years. Some of these efforts still drag on in the courts.

The large logging company that once operated in the forests behind Port Barton, described in the previous chapter as having put San Vicente on the "national map" by attracting prospective logging workers and other migrants, illustrates how the nation's political patronage system intersects with the plunder economy. Jose Alvarez, the company's owner, was once a loyal Marcos supporter and through several companies eventually controlled most commercial logging in Palawan. When Marcos fell, Alvarez successfully realigned himself with Ramon Mitra, a prominent Palawan politician and Marcos foe whose political fortunes were then on the rise. Alvarez also provided free lumber to local army installations, thereby winning the support of the officer commanding the Philippine military in Palawan, and he contributed to the election campaigns of other local politicians. In this way, Alvarez retained control over his logging concessions. In 1988, 2 years after Marcos had fallen and democracy was supposed to have reemerged in the Philippines, Alvarez directly controlled more than half of the logging concessions in northern Palawan, including the one in San Vicente. The wife of the provincial governor, a former governor, a member of the provincial board, and a former town mayor also held concessions in Palawan at that time (Rush 1991: 43).

The Mining Industry

The Philippines is rich in deposits of gold, copper, nickel, and chromite as well as in tropical forests. The history of mining is also marked by political and environmental misbehavior. Extensive gold deposits in the Cordillera Mountains of northern Luzon were worked for generations by indigenous "pocket miners" whose small-scale operations provided a livelihood with minimal environmental damage. In 1903, the Benguet Corporation, a mining company started by U.S. investors and today owned in equal parts by American interests, wealthy Filipinos, and the Philippine government, began exploiting the region's gold deposits and grew to become one of the country's top-twenty corporations and the seventh largest gold producer in the world. Local pocket miners and the Benguet Corporation coexisted peacefully until the early 1980s, when Benguet abandoned its increasingly unprofitable underground mines in favor of open-pit mining. Taking advantage of vast gold-mining concession rights received from the Philippine government, Benguet bulldozed large open-pit mines and encroached upon the pocket mine area without consulting local residents, to the detriment of both local livelihoods and the environment.

Unlike the local pocket miners who use water to separate the gold from the rest of the rock, Benguet uses toxic chemicals, and it flushed those chemicals down the principal river with the mine tailings. Farmers reported that local springs ceased to flow and that cows died from drinking contaminated river water. Farther downstream, rice farmers reported that waterborne mining wastes damaged irrigation canals and caused their rice yields to suffer, and fishermen in the Lingayen Gulf (where the river empties) suffered reductions in their fish catches because of siltation of coral reefs by the tailings. In 1990, displaced pocket miners blockaded the entrance to Keystone West, the most lucrative vein in what Benguet called its "Grand Antamok Project," anticipated to yield the company more than $400 million over its estimated 13-year lifetime. After 3 months, the government intervened, and Benguet agreed to a number of environmental measures including a halt to the dumping of toxins and tailings into the river. After these promises went unfulfilled, the blockade resumed for another year before it ended, although the problems remain. Needing the foreign exchange earnings and tax revenues it receives from Benguet's mining operations, the Philippine government has mostly turned a deaf ear, and local opposition continues to challenge "the right of the few to mine in a fashion so detrimental to the many" (Broad and Cavanagh 1993: 25–31).

In more recent years, the nation's worst industrial disaster unfolded when the largest in a series of toxic spills from a copper mine operated by the Marcopper Mining Corporation caused widespread floods and extensive damage to a number of villages in Marinduque, an island province in southern Luzon. Owned mainly by a Canadian corporation, Placer Dome, Marcopper began operating in Marinduque in 1969 and eventually produced 30 tons of copper ore a day. By 1975, the holding areas constructed by the mine to contain tailings and other wastes had filled, and

Marcopper began to dump mine wastes directly into nearby Calancan Bay. This procedure for tailings disposal is illegal in the United States and Canada but was not then illegal according to Philippine law. By 1991, Marcopper had emptied an estimated 200 million tons of such wastes into the bay, covering corals and sea grasses on an estimated 80 square kilometers of the sea floor and severely affecting the food security of twelve fishing communities. Local residents complained bitterly about the resulting decline in fish catches and demanded that the mine stop dumping tailings into the bay and compensate them for lost fishing income.

Over the years, Marcopper ingratiated itself with the few large landowners and other wealthy individuals who dominated the politics and provincial government of Marinduque by offering them business opportunities to profit from of the mine's operation. With the local power structure firmly in support of continued mining operations, the occasional rulings against the mine that resulted from environmentalist action were overturned in court, and Marcopper continued to empty tailings into Calancan Bay while denying the environmental and human impacts. Then in March 1996, a badly sealed drainage tunnel at the base of the mine burst, and toxic wastes disgorged directly into the nearby Makulapnit and Boac Rivers at the rate of 5 to 10 cubic meters per second. By the time workers contained the toxic spill, an estimated 1.5 million cubic meters or 3 to 4 million tons of mining waste had emptied into the two rivers, causing flash floods that isolated five communities. Six feet of floodwater buried one community; lead contaminated drinking water and killed fish, freshwater shrimp, and pigs; and residents in a third of the province's communities received an advisory notice to evacuate. Government officials declared that the 27-kilometer long Boac River, the main source of livelihood for those who did not work at Marcopper, was biologically dead (Coumans 2002).

The mine shut down amid numerous government investigations, lawsuits, and promises to mitigate the environmental damage. Placer Dome left the Philippines in December 2001, without fulfilling written commitments made to the national government following the 1996 spill to rehabilitate the Boac River and other areas affected by the tailings spill and to compensate local residents for their losses. The move also was in disregard of an October 2001 government order to repair deteriorating dams and other structures that threatened to collapse and cause further environmental damage and human suffering. In short, Placer Dome simply walked away from its responsibilities (Coumans 2002).

A Plunder Economy

Even if one accepts the proposition that humans should exploit natural resources so that they can earn their livings, what has transpired in the Philippines with respect to development and the environment is difficult to accept. Although excessive resource extraction in the Philippines has created employment for people and not just additional wealth for the already-rich, few have benefited, and many have been left out. In 1988, for example, the annual income of Alverez's logging company in San Vicente was $24 million (Rush 1991: 44), a figure more than three times the combined annual income of the approximately 18,000 people who then lived in San Vicente. These people (including logging workers) probably earned annual per capita cash and subsistence incomes on the order of $400 (an estimate based on my fieldwork elsewhere in Palawan during that same year).

Between 1948 and 1987, the Philippines earned billions of U.S. dollars from the export of logs. According to official figures, timber exports peaked in the 1970s and early 1980s at about $200 million per year (Brown 1995), but the actual figures during this period were likely closer to $1 billion a year, with the rest disappearing as abnormally high profits, off-the-books profits and government bribes (Kummer 1992; Repetto 1988).[1] Also between 1948 and 1987, the nation's estimated forest cover declined from 59 percent to 22 percent of total land area (Kummer 2005), because of rampant overcutting and other forms of mismanagement. Many mineral deposits were similarly exhausted during this period. Mineral exports peaked in 1980 at $1.03 billion dollars; they totaled $166 million in 2005 (Buco 2006). Marcopper alone, during its first 20 years in the Philippines, earned more than $1 billion dollars and paid yearly taxes totaling $409 million to the national government (Alibutud 1993).

The greatest tragedy of development and the environment in the Philippines may not be the environmental damage but instead that for the well-being of most of its citizens, the nation has so little to show for billions of dollars of timber sales. From this perspective, no country in Southeast Asia sold off its natural resources more cheaply than did the Philippines.

THE SETTLEMENT AND DEVELOPMENT
OF PALAWAN

The competition to exploit the resources of coastal Palawan is wrapped up with the larger story of the settlement and development of the Palawan region. In 1903, the total population of Palawan was only about 35,000 persons, whereas by 2000, the region's population exceeded 700,000 persons, most of whom resided on Palawan Island (Table 3.1). What brought about this dramatic increase in Palawan's population? Throughout much of the twentieth century, and particularly in the decades following World War II, Palawan's land and other resources beckoned settlers and other migrants from throughout the Philippines. The short version of the story, as I suggested in Chapters 1 and 2, is that global forces caused the island to gradually fill with people. "Global forces," is a broad category, and people involved in the settlement of Palawan and the competition for its resources have varied significantly in the linkages they have with the "outside world." For example, fish from Palawan mostly goes to markets in Manila, whereas minerals go directly to overseas markets.

Chapter 2 showed that within the Palawan region, migrants from Cuyo and Agutaya played a major role in the settlement of Palawan Island. For these migrants from Cuyonon and Agutaynen, their home islands long remained the

TABLE 3.1 Population Growth in the Palawan Region

Philippines	Palawan Province	Palawan Island	San Vicente	
1903	7,635,426	33659	6200	
1918	10,314,310	69053	31863	
1939	16,000,303	93673	44959	
1948	19,234,182	106269	56360	
1960	27,087,685	162669	102540	
1970	36,684,486	236635	162082	5388
1975	42,070,660	300065	214232	7420
1980	48,098,460	317782	269081	10097
1990	60,703,206	528287	400323	17795
2000	76,498,735	755412	601096	21654

SOURCE: National Statistics Office (2000)

centers of gravity—and of "civilization," as they knew it. Palawan was a vast outlier, home of untamed forests, aboriginal peoples, and endemic malaria. Only in the early twentieth century, after Cuyo and Agutaya had filled with people and local agricultural production was no longer sufficient to feed the populations of the two islands, did Cuyonon and Agutaynen residents begin moving to Palawan to meet their subsistence needs. Initially they went as seasonal migrants to plant upland rice in Palawan's fertile, virgin forest soils, and later to settle permanently to farm and to fish. For the peoples of the small islands of the Palawan region, Palawan Island was a resource-rich frontier where rural dwellers could find greater economic opportunity and start life anew, but also where they sought to recreate the lives they had known in their communities of origin.

At the national level, Palawan's vast area came to be settled not only by Cuyonon and Agutaynen and their other small island neighbors, but also by farming and fishing peoples and by Christians and Muslims alike, from throughout the Philippines but particularly (as discussed in Chapter 2) from the Visayan Island region. Between 1960 and 1990, at the height of emigration to Palawan, population growth rates on the island typically exceeded 4 percent per year, a figure well above the rate of natural increase of about 2.4 percent per year. According to the 2000 national census, people in Palawan speak more languages than do people in any other province of the Philippines.

The same basic forces that drove the settlement of older Philippine frontiers in central Luzon, the Cagayan Valley, and Mindanao also drove the settlement of Palawan's frontier. These migrants were usually poor and sought to escape high population density and land and other resource scarcity in long-settled homelands. This much of the national picture resembles the regional picture where migrants originated from nearby Cuyo, faraway Panay in the Visayan Islands or the Ilocos coast in northern Luzon, with similar motives to escape overcrowding and to seek new economic opportunities.

Philippine land frontiers on the national stage have historically served as politically convenient safety valves to relieve some of the pressures caused by government inability or unwillingness to control population growth or to resolve agrarian problems in more densely populated regions (Kerkvliet 1979: 119; Lopez 1987). Further, many of the migrants from these latter locales left to seek greater economic opportunities on Palawan and to escape civil unrest in their communities of origin. Unlike migrants from within the Palawan region, these latter migrants sought peace as well as prosperity in Palawan, and they hoped to establish themselves in Palawan in ways that did not simply recreate the lives they had known back home.

For centuries, and long before Palawan's land and other resources began to affect regional and national economies, Palawan occupied a prominent position in wider Asian trading networks as a source of supply for beeswax, rattan, tree resins, and edible birds' nests. Trade in these and other forest products continues and, as indicated in Chapter 2, is primarily sustained by the labor of Tagbanua and other indigenous peoples. Palawan's significance in the present global economy primarily derives from its considerable timber and mineral resources and, most recently, from its appeal as an international tourist destination.

The logging operation in San Vicente controlled by Jose Alvarez, discussed earlier, was one of many that cut timber in Palawan during the years following World War II until the ban on further logging in 1992. Palawan is home to relatively dry, monsoonal forests of a type known as "molave" forest (Kummer 1992: 43), which contains beautiful and durable hardwoods highly prized in the international markets for furniture manufacture (Bee 1987: 10–11). Mining operations in Palawan, also geared to the demands of world markets, have exploited the island's considerable deposits of chromite, nickel, iron, mercury, manganese, silica sand, talc, and sulfur (Bureau of Mines and Geosciences 1986). When I first arrived in Palawan, one of the largest mercury mines in the world operated on a hillside 15 kilometers from Puerto Princesa City. Among the mines that operate on the island today, the largest belongs to the Rio Tuba Nickel (RTN) Mining Corporation south of Brookes Point. After discovering significant new deposits of nickel, the RTN Corporation recently secured a 20-year extension on its mining permit and announced plans to invest an additional $150 million in its mining operations.

As Palawan has been drawn into this web of regional, national, and global connections, considerable inequalities in wealth, status, and power have emerged among its residents. In contrast with institutionalized class differentiation found in more impoverished and densely inhabited regions of the Philippines, Palawan's agricultural landscape is dominated by smallholding owner-operators, rather than by landlords, and its fishing communities are dominated by small-scale and self-employed fishing peoples, rather than by large commercial fishing companies. Here and there on the coastal plain, zones of coconut and irrigated rice farming have emerged and with them patterns of tenancy and day labor. In the towns, wealthy merchants—some homegrown and some from such places as Manila or Cebu City—control the large-scale trade in produce, fish, and other commodities, and wealthy politicians exert leverage, as they do in other parts of the country, to gain economic advantage.

In the island's rural communities, including those in San Vicente, most immigrant farming and fishing peoples and their descendents fall into the middle and lower reaches of Palawan's wider class structure. Only a relative handful of full-time local residents are even moderately prosperous by the standards of Puerto Princesa City. One reason that few rural residents break into the top tier of the wider class structure is because those who prosper locally tend to move to towns and cities, following the economic or political linkages that made their relative success possible. Such prosperous individuals may maintain a local residence for family or political reasons, but they live and spend most of their time elsewhere. For example, a former mayor of San Vicente ran successfully for an elective provincial office, and he and his family now live most of the time in Puerto Princesa City. Despite these occasional "success stories," class differences between locals and outsiders remain a central feature of the lives of most San Vicente residents.

THE PLUNDER ECONOMY AND
COASTAL PALAWAN

Upon this broader stage of the settlement and development of Palawan, how has the "plunder economy" of the Philippines affected the natural resources of Palawan's coasts? Here briefly are three examples. All involve environmentally damaging resource use practices that violate existing law. Each one illustrates different combinations of involvement by outsiders and local residents and different global linkages.

Illegal Commercial Fishing

One kind of plundering involves the regular intrusions into Palawan waters of trawlers and other large commercial fishing vessels based in Manila and elsewhere in the Philippines. Philippine fisheries produce about 1.8 million tons of fish per year (BFAR 1997). The output from Palawan's fishing grounds, mostly bound for markets in the metropolitan Manila area, account for nearly 40 percent of this total (Valientes 2004). Commercial fishing is legal as long as the trawlers fish in the open sea, but national law reserves waters within 15 kilometers of the coast for the exclusive use of fishermen from local municipalities. In Palawan as elsewhere in the country, large commercial fishing boats often enter municipal waters illegally in search of fish. They employ highly efficient but environmentally damaging fishing gear (see, e.g., Russell and Alexander 2000; Sunderlin and Gorospe 1997). One widely used and particularly destructive gear is the Danish seine. This gear makes use of a weighted and motorized scare line dragged across the ocean bottom or over a coral reef to herd fish into a fixed net several kilometers in length. Commercial fishing vessels remain out of sight from the shore, but their powerful electrical systems light up the horizon at night for all to see. The operators of these vessels reportedly pay off mayors and other local officials to ensure that their illegal activities go unchallenged. A significant amount of local resource depletion and the associated decline in local fish catches in Palawan is the result of illegal commercial fishing by outsiders.

Who count as "outsiders" and what constitutes "local" resources are always relative questions. An international dimension arises here because the fishing vessels of other countries in the region, particularly China, regularly enter and fish in Philippine territorial waters, in violation of international treaties and agreements. Several times in recent years, the Philippine Coast Guard has confiscated Chinese boats caught fishing in Palawan waters, and on at least one occasion, an entire fishing crew spent several weeks in jail in Puerto Princesa City. When I was last in Palawan, the Coast Guard chased, boarded, and detained a Chinese fishing vessel that had captured more than a hundred sea turtles, valuable in China for their shells, in violation of Philippine law and international treaty. Local media accounts talked about how Palawan residents had disciplined themselves not to eat turtle meat anymore only to have Chinese come and capture the turtles so that they could decorate their homes with the shells. In December 2006, park rangers guarding Palawan's Tubbataha Reef Marine Park arrested thirty Chinese fishermen with 800 live fish they had caught inside the park. The occasional detention of Chinese fishing boats notwithstanding, most of such boats are likely to enter and fish in Philippine waters undetected because of the military's limited capacity to patrol those waters on a regular basis. The incursions of Chinese fishing boats pose a foreign policy dilemma for the Philippines, which is anxious to maintain cordial diplomatic relations with its more powerful neighbor.

Cyanide Fishing and the Live Fish Trade

A second kind of plundering of coastal resources occurs in association with the live fish trade. This trade centers on the raising to market size highly prized species of fish in pens or cages, much as a farmer might fatten a pig before sale. The raft-like floating cages range from 5 to 10 meters on a side and are located in protected bays and inlets free of pollution (see Figure 3.1). The fish are fed until they reach about 1 kilogram in size, before being collected and shipped live to Manila, by boat or plane, for export to restaurants in Hong Kong. The fish most commonly raised for this trade in Palawan are various kinds of groupers and wrasses. Fishermen occasionally harvest adults of these species while hook-and-line fishing. Fishermen often bring along a basin or ice chest in which to store live fish in seawater and transport them back to shore. A fisherman "hits the jackpot" by capturing a grouper or wrasse. In 2006, local fishermen and fish-cage operators received about $30 per kilogram for Napoleon wrasse later sold to patrons of restaurants in Hong Kong and Taiwan for as much as $80 per kilogram. The live fish trade is an important industry with an estimated annual retail value of $1 billion in the Asia-Pacific region, $30 million in the Philippines, and $18 million in Palawan (PCSD 2005). Approximately one hundred fish pens currently operate in Palawan, including several in San Vicente.

Courtesy of James F. Eder

FIGURE 3.1 A fish pen for raising grouper at Panindigan

As with the illegal intrusions of commercial fishing vessels into municipal waters, the primary beneficiaries of the live fish trade are wealthy business people who live elsewhere. However, in the live fish trade, some local fishermen are also involved either as caretakers of the pens or as suppliers of young live fish. The latter activity draws accusations of causing environmental damage and resource plunder. Juvenile fish needed to stock the pens must be caught in the wild, and the most common capture technique involves the use of sodium cyanide. The procedure is simple and destructive. Sometimes holding his breath but usually employing a hookah rig attached to an air compressor, a cyanide fisherman descends onto a coral reef and, after spotting a likely fish, uses a baby feeding bottle to squirt the cyanide into the coral hiding place where his prey character-istically retreats. The cyanide stuns the fish and makes them easier to catch, although it is sometimes necessary to tear apart the coral to retrieve the fish from their hiding places. The juvenile fish thus captured and stored in Styrofoam ice chests filled with seawater are delivered to the pen operators for sale. Meanwhile, the cyanide kills nearby fish roe and coral polyps and eventually bleaches reefs. For these reasons, the law prohibits cyanide use. (Fish caught with cyanide soon excrete it and are not likely pose a danger to human consumers.)

Pen operators deny that they use cyanide in their fishing operations. Defen-ders of the live fish trade advocate catching the young fish by hook-and-line and have conducted demonstrations to show that it can be done. Most knowledge-able observers argue that it is extremely difficult to use hook-and-line to catch significant numbers of the principal species and that the trade would not remain profitable without the use of cyanide. Despite a continuing public campaign to educate fishermen about the environmental and livelihood costs of cyanide use, the practice continues. Damage to coral reefs from the use of cyanide in the Palawan region is extensive, and official recognition of that damage led, in 1993, to a 5-year ban on catching and shipping live fish from the province. Under pressure from wealthy business interests, the province did not renew the ban, but several municipalities (not including San Vicente) currently have their own bans in place.

Blast Fishing

The third kind of plunder is by local fishermen engaged in affecting coastal resources on their own, again in violation of the law, but without any elite support or protection. The most conspicuous example of the misbehavior of local fishermen is blast fishing. Blast or dynamite fishing has a long history in the Philippines, and it remains a serious problem throughout the country. The explosives come from military personnel, mining workers, and other sources. In its crudest form, blast fishermen light a stick of dynamite or other explosive and toss it into the middle of a school of fish. Sometimes they set out palm fronds and other fish aggregating devices to increase the catch from a targeted blast. The shock wave from a blast stuns or kills most fish in the vicinity and causes significant collateral damage, particularly to coral reefs. During my years in Palawan, I have sometimes been on the beach or out to sea at night and heard blast fishermen at work off in the distance; I always found the experience profoundly discomforting. Other forms of blast fishing involve setting and detonating explosives at various depths, which makes blast fishermen more difficult to detect but is equally damaging. Most consumers can recognize fish caught with explosives; the flesh is softer and the eyes are often discolored. For these reasons such fish command lower prices in the marketplace, but shoppers purchase them, and blast fishing remains profitable for those who pursue it.

How extensive is the damage to Palawan's coral reefs caused by cyanide use, blast fishing, and other human impacts? Concerns about this and other environmental damage caused by the plunder of Palawan's resources led in 1992 to the passage into national law of a strategic environmental plan (SEP) for the island. The SEP provides for the eventual zoning of all of Palawan into an environmentally critical areas network (ECAN) intended to provide for controlled, environmentally sound development on land and in coastal areas. The Palawan Council for Sustainable Development (PCSD), an agency of the national government, is responsible for implementing the SEP. Specifically, the council should use ECAN zoning to protect vulnerable areas; control development activities in the province through the use of environmental impact assessments; intensify agricultural development in lowland areas to relieve human pressures on the uplands; and foster sustainable use of common resources by local communities. Palawan is the only province in the Philippines to have such a nationally mandated environmental protection plan.

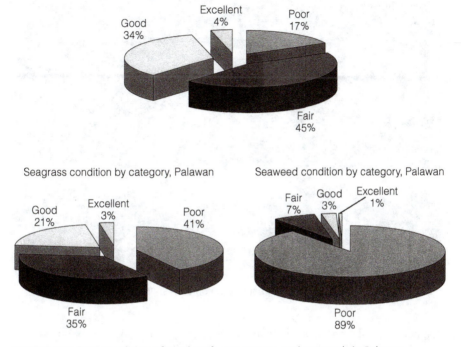

F I G U R E 3.2   Condition of coral reefs, sea grasses, and seaweeds in Palawan

Figure 3.2 displays the results of a 1999 study of the condition of 305 coral reefs in Palawan by the staff of the Palawan Council for Sustainable Development. Figure 3.2 shows that only about 40 percent of the reefs surveyed are in excellent or good condition, whereas 60 percent are in fair or poor condition. Figure 3.2 also displays the findings of the same study on the condition of various sea grass and seaweed communities around Palawan, two other coastal resources that have been ever more negatively impacted by the use of cyanide and explosives.

NEW GLOBAL DEMANDS ON COASTAL
SAN VICENTE

The plunder of coastal Palawan was not an orchestrated or a one-time event, as these examples show. It is an ongoing process that involves many actors, big and small. The global forces that drive this plunder are not all uniformly distributed across Palawan. The intrusions of commercial fishing vessels into municipal waters and the destructive fishing practices of blast fishermen occur just about anywhere. Other global forces, such as those that bring tourists to the Philippines in search of adventure or foreigners in search of retirement homes, have

Courtesy of James F. Eder

FIGURE 3.3   A European retirement home on Buayan Island

distinctive local impacts in their interaction with local resources, opportunities, and constraints. Next, I show how new global influences have affected particular coastal resources in San Vicente.

Foreigners and Their Doings

Most people from outside the Philippines who visit San Vicente go there as tourists, but several dozen "foreigners"—including Germans, Swiss, Canadians, Australians, Americans, and other outsiders—have put down a variety of seasonal or permanent roots. A retired French businessman has built his dream home on an idyllic cove on Buayan Island (Figure 3.3). On the opposite side of the same cove lies an artist colony established by a Filipino American woman from San Francisco. A Canadian woman, acting largely on her own, has attempted to establish a marine turtle sanctuary by declaring the waters in front of her beach property at Imuruan Island to be off-limits to fishing. An American missionary couple in New Agutaya and a Polish missionary couple near Binga translate and teach the New Testament in local languages. A German woman who is a skilled scuba diver operates a diving business catering to tourists in Port Barton.

Foreigners have varied reputations—some are friendly, others not. Locals widely disliked the woman who attempted to establish a turtle sanctuary. They said she "loves turtles more than people." She once forced several fishermen to empty their nets at gunpoint and was later tried in court for the incident. The artist colony, for want of a better term, seemed closed and almost cult-like to me, and I felt badly out of place when I attempted a visit. Some foreigners employ local residents to help with household chores, and missionaries come specifically to interact with local residents and make converts. Most local people still have little or no sustained contact with foreigners, other than tourists, but these foreigners inexorably influence local economy and society even if they at times appear to be living in a "parallel universe."

Residents of San Vicente most prominently associate foreigners with the purchase of beachfront property. As a foreigner myself, albeit of a kind that local residents found difficult to categorize, I have received countless inquiries asking if I would like to buy a beach. At first, and because of San Vicente's relative remoteness, I assumed that only the occasional adventuresome foreigner might buy local property. One of my most startling research findings was that more than half of San Vicente's prime beachfront property, both along the coast and on the various offshore islands, is under the ownership of foreigners and a handful of wealthy provincial politicians. Some foreign owners have built retirement homes or small private resorts for entertaining friends, but most reside abroad or live elsewhere in the Philippines. These absentee owners acquired the land for investment purposes or because they plan someday to retire and build on it or to construct a beach resort of their own.

I was surprised to realize how much beach property has passed into foreign hands, and I was astounded to discover what beach property today costs. If you think you would like to own some of this property, an Internet search of beaches for sale in Palawan will quickly turn up attractive properties, but be prepared to pay for them. The price of one beach parcel in San Vicente measuring 200 meters long and 200 meters back from the beach was $75,000. This price was low compared with that of beach property on the West Coast of the United States, but such prices were extremely expensive from the perspective of local residents, none of whom could possibly afford to buy beach property today. If you would like to buy an entire island, you can find one for sale as well. One such place, Double Island, I visited inadvertently because the boat I had hired for the day experienced engine trouble and we put ashore to look for a tow. The island's caretaker told me that the owner, a wealthy Filipino businessman, lived in Vancouver, Canada and was thinking of selling the island for 100 million pesos, or about two million U.S. dollars. (He asked if I might be interested.) The island was 17 hectares in area, partially planted in coconut palms, and had several nice stretches of beach, although most of the shoreline was rocky or in mangroves. Three tenant families would remain on the island. I suppose that in some circles, this island would be something of a bargain, but not in mine!

Destination Palawan!

The image of Palawan on the national stage has changed dramatically in recent decades. When I first arrived in the Philippines, most Filipinos I met knew Palawan only for the island's endemic malaria and the presence of a penal colony and a leprosarium, both of which date to the American colonial period. Today, the national images are more positive, though similarly simplistic: Palawan, the "last frontier;" Palawan, "a land of unspoiled natural beauty." To a significant degree, Palawan is these things, and throughout the island, places of interest beckon tourists. A remarkable underground river, 8 kilometers in length, courses under the rugged limestone and marble cliffs of Yosemite-like Mt. St. Paul in the Puerto Princesa Subterranean River National Park, a UNESCO World Heritage site. The river empties into an idyllic lagoon on the west coast of Palawan. Another World Heritage site, the Tubbataha Reef Marine Park (mentioned earlier) offers scuba divers the best diving in insular Southeast Asia. The Tabon Caves Complex, near the southern town of Quezon, yielded a rich trove of cultural artifacts belonging to different cultural chronologies ranging from tens of thousands of years ago to the fourteenth century A.D. Here, archaeologists recovered the skeletal remains of "Tabon Man," recently dated to 40,000 years ago and one of the oldest *Homo sapiens* finds in Southeast Asia. The best known and most expensive tourist resorts are located in northern Palawan, particularly El Nido, the setting for an episode of the popular American television program *The Amazing Race,* filmed against the area's dramatic seaside cliffs.

San Vicente's tourist industry is more modest and consists of a string of about ten small beach resorts lying on Port Barton Bay. These resorts opened during the 1970s and 1980s, when the logging company described in Chapter 2 began operating in Port Barton and constructed a logging road to connect its sawmill with the national highway on the east side of the Palawan. Port Barton's resorts cater mostly to off-the-beaten track, budget travelers. Beach cottages rent for $10 to 20 per night, and for the price, they are quite comfortable. Visitors can easily hire a boat from a local fisherman to visit the various small islands and diving sites in the bay. Foreign expatriates own some resorts, which bear names that suggest their countries of origin (Figure 3.4). Several of the resorts have their own websites, but most rely on word-of-mouth or the various resort listings that appear on tourist-oriented websites to attract visitors. With road access still difficult and tourist traffic highly seasonal, Port Barton's resorts together only receive a few thousand visitors each year.

During my field research in San Vicente, I twice stayed at a beach resort in Port Barton, to see what they were like and to combine business with pleasure. At one of the resorts, I met Dan, whom I came to know as Dan the Bartender or Dan the Chicago White Sox fan. Dan was originally from Chicago and the son of a man who had founded a successful nursery business there. When his father died, Dan (who had previously visited Port Barton as a tourist) sold the business, moved to Port Barton, and partnered with a local woman to open a beach resort. The resort did not seem particularly prosperous when I visited, but it received enough business to support the owners in relative comfort. Dan seemed quite happy living in Port Barton and told me that he has never regretted his decision to leave Chicago, although his memories of home were clearly fond enough that he named the resort's bar the "Chicago Sunset Water Hole" and decorated it with White Sox paraphernalia.

The municipal government of San Vicente and many present and prospective resort operators correctly recognize the unrealized tourism potential in the area. In addition to beautiful beaches, swimming, and snorkeling, it boasts of several outstanding waterfalls at short distances from the coast, a sizeable, river-

Courtesy of James F. Eder

FIGURE 3.4   The Swissippini beach resort at Port Barton

mouth mangrove forest, and a heron sanctuary. Beaches remain the main attractions for most tourists, and tourists can find beaches in abundance elsewhere on Palawan and in the Philippines. In this regard, San Vicente faces considerable competition, and even more now because municipalities throughout the province are attempting to lure tourists with similar suites of attractions. Locals engage in heady local talk about the future. The mayor is presently lobbying for funding to expand the present airport, which is currently used primarily to fly out live fish in private planes, to receive commercial air traffic direct from Manila, so that tourists will not have to travel overland from Puerto Princesa City. The wealthy former operator of the logging concession has a still more ambitious plan. He hopes to open a five-star resort on his property on Port Barton Bay and to construct an international airport where high-end tourists could arrive directly from abroad by private plane. So far, however, this is just talk about how already well-off people might make money from tourism.

Privatizing Coastal Resources

The longer I stayed in San Vicente, the more I appreciated the breadth and depth of the demands that outside people and outside enterprises place on San Vicente's coastal resources. I knew that outsiders wanted fish and squid from San Vicente, but later I also learned that they wanted lobsters, prawns, and sea cucumbers.

I never heard about some local resources sought by outsiders, as they never surfaced in conversations, and I never thought to ask about them. Instead, I stumbled upon them in the course of my fieldwork. One day I was walking along the beach from one community to another, and I came upon an excavation in the sand. It was an excavation that a large group of children playing together might think to make. Then I encountered other such excavations, perhaps twenty or thirty in all. When I inquired, I learned that a group of men had come to collect beach pebbles, popular with well-to-do urban and suburban dwellers for decorating concrete walkways and patios. Apparently they filled and hauled away many sacks of pebbles before municipal authorities noticed their activities. Rather than pay for the necessary municipal permit, the men disappeared. Most local residents had no idea that a government permit to collect pebbles from the beach was even necessary, nor could they imagine why people elsewhere might want to buy them. Tony, the migrant fisherman I introduced in the last chapter, found the idea of "owning your own rocks," particularly amusing. "Some people must have a lot of money," was the only explanation that he could offer.

Another day I came upon a group of large boats pulled ashore, all carrying traps of a type I had never seen before. When I stopped to investigate, I learned that the crews had collected thousands of nautilus shells for shipment to Japan. Japanese discard the meat of the shell but collectors covet the shell.

Once I was visiting a remote bay and came upon a boat and a group of divers in the middle of a huge school of jellyfish, of a type harmless to humans but prized as a food in Japan. The divers were collecting the jellyfish for sale and subsequent export. Here too, local residents wondered aloud to me why anyone would want to buy or own such seemingly innocuous and limitless resources as seashells and jellyfish. Tony joked that if the shell collectors ever returned, he intended to ask to see their shell-collecting permit, even if he had no idea whether such a permit was necessary.

Some coastal resources are valuable in enhancing other resources before sale. The growing use of fish pens to raise prized varieties of fish for the live fish trade is an example. Even if only in a small way, fish pens privatize parts of the ocean. In San Vicente, a substantial part of Port Barton Bay contains a large pearl farm, begun in the mid-1990s with Japanese capital but now in Filipino hands. The pearls, the oyster-like shells in which they are cultured, and the meat of those shells are exported to Japan. Port Barton Marine Products Corporation, which presently operates the farm, holds a long-term lease from the municipal government for several square kilometers of the bay. The corporation's annual lease payment is an important component of municipal revenue. The pearl farm occupies a part of the bay previously frequented by poor fisherman using oar-powered boats. This area is now closed to fishing.

Conflicts arise between different globally driven uses as well as between global and local uses. For example, the tourist industry relies on the presence of pristine coral reefs to attract tourists interested in snorkeling and diving. To the degree that the use of cyanide in the live fish trade damages local reefs, such tourists will presumably stop coming. Resort operators also worry about the growing privatization of the most attractive beaches that attract tourists. Despite nominal private ownership, beaches in the Philippines for a long time were legally and culturally considered open access resources, and anyone could put ashore and use them for the day. Today, with the rise in value of beach property and the shift of that property into elite and foreign hands, growing numbers of "private property" and "keep out" signs have begun to appear, and a few of the wealthiest owners have even hired guards or caretakers to discourage casual visitors.

THE FUTURE OF NATURAL RESOURCE USE IN THE PHILIPPINES

The remaining chapters of this volume will explore in greater detail coastal resource use in San Vicente and consider what might be done to put coastal resource use there on a sounder social and environmental footing. What lessons should we carry forward to that effort from what I have presented here about natural resource use in Palawan and in the Philippines? First, many of the principal exploiters of local coastal resources live elsewhere and remain largely out of local sight. This circumstance poses a challenge to fieldwork. I tried repeatedly and unsuccessfully to interview the owner of the fish pen in Figure 3.1. He maintained a local residence but spent most of his time in Manila. The problem is not insurmountable, and the main lesson is to be aware of the potential importance of unseen actors and to seek indirect ways of finding out about their activities.

Second, "outsiders" and "rich people" are not the only ones who abuse natural resources; some local residents do too, especially the poor. Anthropologists tend to be sympathetic to the plight of poor people and are inclined to give them the benefit of the doubt or to excuse environmental misbehavior by calling attention to their poverty or other extenuating circumstances. Local residents who abuse coastal resources argue with some justification that everyone, and not just rich people, should be free to advance their own economic positions, and if the wealthy can do this by "plundering" coastal resources, why not poor people as well? I heard this argument repeatedly from local fishermen. In a national economy that has long suffered from underemployment and unemployment, the argument that everyone should have the opportunity to support themselves and their families by whatever honest and hard-working means they can find has considerable cultural and moral weight. In recent years, the message that "God put natural resources on earth for man to use," spoken by local church leaders, resonates with the daily concerns of congregation members who repeated this message to me to defend their resource use practices and criticize those who sought to change them. At the same time most local fishermen, including many who are poor, do not employ cyanide or explosives to exploit coastal resources.

Third, the Philippine state historically has been a weak and even inept manager of its natural resources, unable to enforce laws against use of cyanide and explosives in fishing and equally unable to regularly catch Chinese boats fishing in territorial waters The weakness of the state has had other significant consequences of a positive nature in ceding substantial space to such nongovernmental organizations as Conservation International and World Wildlife Fund to undertake local resource management programs of their own.[2]

Fourth, a significant problem facing any new state-sponsored resource management effort is that the government's past failure to manage resource extraction on a sustainable and socially just basis has engendered considerable cynicism among local residents regarding its present abilities and intentions. Allegations of mismanagement and corruption in government agencies and programs—including natural resource management programs—routinely appear in investigative reports in national newspapers and on "talk radio" programs in Puerto Princesa City. San Vicente residents hear and repeat these allegations, particularly when they are connected with the politics of plunder. Some repeated them to me or had stories of their own to tell about government misbehavior, and most local residents are quite cynical about officials at all levels of government. "They're all corrupt," they told me, as if that was all one needed to know about them. New natural resource management programs and policies, however well-intended, will need to overcome this cynicism if they are to gain local support and cooperation.

ENDNOTES

1.   The government's own Commission on Audit estimated that between 1975 and 1980, 10 percent of the nation's entire GNP went to bribes (Tapales 1986).

2.   These and other international environmentalist organizations have long been active in Palawan, but none currently have programs or projects in San Vicente.

4

Making a Living in a
Coastal Ecosystem

This chapter is about the economic lives of the ordinary people who compose the great bulk of San Vicente's population. Some are like the caretaker of the fish pen in Figure 3.1, people I sometimes thought of as wage-earning proletarians in the world capitalist system, employed directly by the global economy to raise specialized fish and farm produce that they could never afford to buy. Most fishing and farming men and women in San Vicente, however, still work for themselves, and they participate in or are influenced by the global economy in less direct ways. They must compete with each other to earn their livings in a setting where the powerful outside business interests and other global economic forces discussed in the previous chapter threaten to further erode the coastal resources on which they must rely. We may also think of the subjects of this chapter as they sometimes think of themselves, as the "small people" who are the backbone of Philippine economic life but whose interests and concerns are consistently overshadowed by "big people," such as the logging baron or the fish pen owner described in Chapter 3.

Households are the basic units of production and consumption in the Philippines. I begin by explaining household organization and calling attention to the important role that women play in the economic life of households in rural communities. Drawing on my household surveys in two San Vicente communities, I discuss the ownership of fishing boats and nets, farmland and farm animals, and other productive assets; the occupations of household members; and the incomes that households receive from their various productive activities.

The second part of the chapter concerns how the individual members of households go about the everyday business of making a living from fishing, farming, and other activities. Here, I report what I learned by talking to fishermen about their boats and their gear, about the composition of crews, about favored fishing grounds, and about how they share and sell fish. This book is primarily about fishing and the men and women who rely upon it for their livings, but we can understand fishing only in the context of farming and other coastal zone livelihoods because these various livelihoods are interdependent, within and between households. In the second part of the chapter, I briefly consider farming and other livelihoods.

In the last part of the chapter, I show how individual households in San Vicente adjust their livelihood strategies to cope with the global forces discussed in Chapter 3, forces that have brought both new difficulties and new opportunities to local residents. On the one hand, relentless exploitation of coastal resources, diminishing returns to time spent fishing and the rising price of gasoline have made it more difficult to survive by fishing alone. On the other hand, global interconnections in some cases have suggested new and potentially more remunerative ways of making a living.

HOUSEHOLD ECONOMIC LIFE

The fishing and farming people who compose the population of San Vicente are householders, groups of individuals living together under a common roof and sharing a variety of household tasks. Households in general engage in some combination of production, distribution (sharing, consumption, and saving), biological and social reproduction, transmission of property, and co-residence (Netting 1993: 59). Households often consist of families that may vary considerably in form—they may be nuclear families or extended families, they may be male-headed or female-headed, and so on. The shared, quasi-corporate nature of a household's characteristic activities is the most characteristic feature. The family household mobilizes and allocates the labor and manages the resources of the household, and it is the key productive unit in most rural societies (Netting 1993: 100–101).

Households in the Philippines are almost always families, and this powerfully influences the ways households function as productive enterprises, particularly with regard to how they allocate labor and resources. According to Netting, "The key relationships that order the social world of the family—parent/child, older/younger, female/male, brother/sister—simultaneously structure both social and moral expectations and provide a conduit for environmental knowledge, task skills, and modes of labor organization" (1993: 63). The distinctive and goal-oriented ways whereby households organize their labor and other resources have led many observers to speak of them as having self-conscious and quasi-corporate "livelihood strategies," and I employ this notion in this chapter. We must also pay careful attention to what goes on inside households, for such crucial variables as age, gender, authority, and cultural principles of behavior influence the interests and activities of individual members (Barlett 1989; Wilk 1991). In short, the household and the individuals within it are not identical and interchangeable units. In the end, "households" do not decide things, people do—and, more particularly, certain people rather than others (Wolf 1991: 14, 30). I pay special attention in this chapter to the role of gender in household decision-making that surrounds the formulation and implementation of household economic strategies.

TABLE 4.1 Ownership of Productive Assets in Panindigan and New Agutaya

Number of households owning assets in:

Asset:	40 Panindigan households	40 New Agutaya households
Motorized boat	25	2
Oar-powered boat	12	8
Fishing net	24	4
Hook and line	38	8
Squid jigger	14	0
Irrigated rice land	3	31
Other land	8	15
Water buffalo	0	18
Cow	0	12
Pig	12	38
Plow	1	27
Store	3	4
Rice mill	1	4

First, I return to the two household surveys discussed in Chapter 2, of the fishing community of Panindigan and the farming community of New Agutaya. What does information from these surveys show about household economic life in San Vicente?

Table 4.1 concerns the major productive assets in these two communities: boats and nets in the case of fishing households, and land and farm animals in the case of farming households. Table 4.1 shows that in the forty households surveyed in Panindigan, most households own either a motorized or an oar-powered fishing boat, and more than half of the households own a fishing net (a few owned several boats, or more than one net). In New Agutaya, most households own both farmland, either irrigated or rain-fed, and farm animals. The numbers of animals and the amount of farmland owned varies between households. Of the thirty-one households in New Agutaya that own irrigated rice land, most own between 1 and 2 hectares, several owned only a half hectare, and a few owned 6 or more hectares.

Table 4.1 also shows that the associations of households in Panindigan with fishing and households in New Agutaya with farming are not uniform. Some Panindigan households keep pigs, and a number of New Agutaya households own fishing boats. Table 4.2 presents information on primary and secondary income sources in both communities, showing that households in San Vicente often rely on multiple economic activities for their incomes. I gathered this information in response to the questions, "What is the most important source of income in this household?" and "Are there other important sources of income

T A B L E 4.2 Primary and Secondary Income Sources
in Panindigan and New Agutaya

Number of households reporting in:

	40 Panindigan households	40 New Agutaya households
Primary income source:		
Fishing	33	
Drying fish	2	
Buying/selling fish	1	
Rice farming		34
Piggery	1	3
Share harvesting		2
Carpentry	1	
Store owner	2	1
Secondary income source:		
Fishing	3	14
Drying fish	5	
Buying/selling fish	3	
Piggery	4	7
Day care provider	1	
Avon dealer	1	
Seaweed farming	4	
Thatch making	1	2
Rice mill	1	2
Pastor	1	
Store owner	1	3
Share harvesting	3	5

in this household?" Though some households are totally dependent on a single source of income, most households in both communities receive income from a second source. Though fishing or some fishing-related activity is the primary income source for almost all households in Panindigan, some earn supplementary incomes from agricultural activities, and in many of the farming households in New Agutaya, fishing is an important secondary activity.

During my fieldwork, one U.S. dollar was worth about fifty Philippine pesos, and one peso was worth approximately U.S. $0.02. With this conversion in mind and looking at the mean income figures, annual household cash income in both communities is about $1,000 per year.

Differences between households in the number or size of their fishing boats, in the amount of farmland land they own, and in how many sources of income

TABLE 4.3 Annual Cash Incomes in Panindigan and New Agutaya (pesos)

	40 Panindigan households	40 New Agutaya households
For households in:		
Upper third	73,000	102,200
Middle third	43,800	51,100
Lower third	25,550	32,850
Mean	47,450	62,050

they have indicate that households in both communities must vary considerably in the amount of income they receive. Table 4.3 displays, in Philippine pesos, the estimated annual cash incomes for the sample households in Panindigan and New Agutaya, grouping together households in the upper, middle, and lower thirds (Table 4.3 does not account for fish caught and consumed at home, or the rice and other agricultural goods that farmers produce and consume at home. I estimate that such "subsistence income," composes half or more of total household income in many households in these two communities.) As expected, Table 4.3 shows considerable variation between households in the amounts of cash income they receive. In both Panindigan and New Agutaya, households in the upper third receive about three times as much income as households in the lower third. Households here and elsewhere in San Vicente vary considerably in their economic security and well-being, even if in terms of the "big people"/ "small people" contrast, all of the households discussed here are in the "small people" category.

The data on household economic life obtained from my surveys raised numerous questions needing additional research. "Fishing" embraced many different activities and kinds of equipment that I would need to investigate. For example, what difference did it make if a household owned a motorized or an oar-powered fishing boat? How did fishing nets vary in size and purpose? How could a household receive income from fishing but own neither a boat nor a net? Similar questions suggested themselves about farming. How could a household primarily engaged in farming also receive income from fishing? What about all those secondary occupations in Table 4.2? Where exactly do women figure in all of this? These are among the questions I explore in this chapter.

LIVELIHOODS IN THE COASTAL ZONE

Fishing

The fieldwork experience I recounted in Chapter 1, when I walked onto the beach in San Vicente and found it teeming with beach seiners, later proved atypical, for when I later visited the beachfront, I usually found far fewer people.

What I did find in abundance was fishing boats. Large and small, of different colors and with sometimes amusing names, boats were everywhere, and one of the surest ways to meet a fisherman was to hang around his boat. Often, the owner would soon appear, not so much suspicious of my presence as curious about why I would be interested in his boat. I found it easy to meet people and make new friends by talking about boats, much as two Americans might get to know one another by talking about their cars. I would ask questions about the boat—how old was it, how big was the engine, where was it made, and if I could take a photograph of it. All of my initial questions were non-invasive and easier to pose than the more personal questions that I hoped ask on another day such as catch size and income from fishing.

I traveled widely by various kinds of boats in the Palawan region. Often, it is still the only way to get somewhere, and at one time, I even had my own outrigger canoe. I traveled many times by boat in San Vicente, sometimes for hours at a time, either because I joined family outings to an island beach or because I hitched a ride or hired a boat to travel to a distant community. However, I rarely accompanied fishermen on their fishing trips. Direct observations of fishing were not central to my research. I found it difficult not to be in the way of the crew, and perhaps more than anything, I found fishing trips to be too tedious and tiring. I have hiked extensively throughout Palawan, and I thought I had encountered significant physical hardship crossing rivers and tramping through tropical forests, but I decided it was harder to sit on a fishing boat all night long with no place to lie down!

The boats themselves are of a type common to small-scale fishermen and other coastal dwellers throughout island Southeast Asia. Their construction is entirely of wood, plywood, bamboo, and rattan. Long, narrow, and with substantial bamboo outriggers, fishing boats are incredibly seaworthy. Several times out at sea, I ran into severe storms, but returned safely to shore despite heavy rain and large swells that would have prompted small craft warnings along the southern California coast. The larger boats are known as "pumpboats" (*pambots*) and have small gasoline engines. Most common are 5 and 10 horsepower engines, the former to power boats approximately 20 feet in length used mainly for hook-and-line or squid fishing, and the latter to power the pumpboats needed to deploy fishing nets. Despite the small size of their engines, the boats are shallow-drafted and can move along at a good clip. The smaller boats, known as *bancas,* are oar-powered and are sometimes rigged with a sail, although lacking a keel, they are limited to running with the wind (Figures 4.1 and 4.2). A new pumpboat of medium size today costs about U.S. $1,000; a new *banca* costs $100 to 200.

Fishermen typically go out singly or in pairs to fish with a hook and line or to catch squid using a piece of equipment known as a "jig" or "jigger," which is continuously lowered and raised from the boat (Figure 4.3). For net fishing, crews of two or three are common, depending on the size of the net. Nets vary widely in length, mesh size, and purpose. Most are hundreds of meters in length, and new ones cost $100 to 300, depending on the size and type. Fishermen take considerable care with their nets' use and storage. Nets also vary according to whether they are intended to sink or to float once they are

Courtesy of James F. Eder

FIGURE 4.1 A fisherman and his pumpboat at Alimanguan

Courtesy of James F. Eder

FIGURE 4.2 A farmer's *banca* at New Canipo

Courtesy of James F. Eder

F I G U R E 4.3 A fisherman's squid-jigging equipment

set. Fishermen typically characterize their nets according to the kind of fish they catch (Tables 4.4 and 4.5). Most gill nets are known by the generic term *lambat* (Table 4.5), but they are further distinguished according to mesh size and the name of a fish. For example, a gill net with a relatively fine mesh may be referred to as a *lambat pang-sapsap,* a net for slipmouth, whereas one with a large mesh may be called a *lambat pang-tanguingue,* a net for the highly prized but rarely caught Spanish mackerel.

Net fishing also varies according to how "efficient" or "active" it is. This variation is the result of the types of nets, and how fishermen deploy them. Efficiency is not entirely a good thing in this context. A fine-meshed net will catch more fish than one with a larger mesh, but some of the fish are likely to be juveniles and too small to be useful to humans. For this reason, the national Fisheries Code of 1998 bans the use of nets with a mesh size less than 3 cm, except to take designated species such as anchovies, which remain small even when mature.

T A B L E 4.4 Commonly Caught Fish in San Vicente

Local name	Common English name	Scientific name
bisugo	threadfin bream	*Nemipterus sp.*
dilis	anchovy	*Stolephorus, Thryssa sp.*
hasa-hasa	short-bodied mackerel	*Rastrelliger brachysoma*
kanuping	emperor bream	*Lethrinus sp.*
lapu-lapu	grouper	*Epinephelus, Plectropomus sp.*
matambaka	big-eyed scad	*Selar crumenophthalmus*
salayginto	yellow-striped crevalle	*Caranx leptolepsis*
salimburao	Indian mackerel	*Rastrelliger kanagurta*
sapsap	slipmouth; ponyfish	*Leiognathus sp.*
talakitok	jack	*Carangidae sp.*
tambakol	skipjack tuna	*Katsuwonus pelamis*
tamban	sardine	*Sardinella aurita*
tulingan	frigate tuna	*Auxis thazard*

SOURCE: San Vicente (2001)

T A B L E 4.5 Commonly Used Fishing Techniques in San Vicente

Technique	Common English term	Target fish
pangawil	hook-and-line	grouper; jack
timing	hook-and-line	threadfin bream; emperor bream
subid	long line	frigate tuna; skipjack tuna
bitana	beach seine	slipmouth
lambat	gill net	crevalle; sardine; slipmouth; Spanish mackerel
pamo	drift gill net	big-eyed scad; mackerel
kurantay	encircling gill net	any small schooling fish
talakop	ring net	any small schooling fish
panti	throw net	any small schooling fish
ganti-ganti	squid jigger	squid
baklad	fish corral	rabbitfish
bubo	fish trap/cage	grouper
panak	crab trap/cage	crab
tangkal	stationary life net	anchovy; slipmouth
pamana	spear-fishing	snapper; grouper

Active gear catches fish by trapping or encirclement, and is more efficient than passive gear, such as a stationary gill net or a hook-and-line dropped and left in place to wait for fish to swim into harm's way. Baby trawls and modified Danish seines are examples of active gear used by some fishermen in San Vicente. A trawl is a cone-shaped net towed along the seafloor to catch slipmouth, threadfin bream, and other bottom-dwelling fish. This fishing technique is characteristic of large commercial fishing boats (or "trawlers"), but as the name *baby trawl* implies, local fishermen have adopted a smaller-scale version. In another local version of the trawl, the *galadgad,* fishermen drag a wooden board along the bottom (Austin 2003: 189). A modified Danish seine, known locally as a *hulbot-hulbot,* is yet another smaller-scale version of a technique used by commercial fishing boats, the Danish seine. Fishermen spread out a net in a pear shape on the ocean floor and keep the boat in a fixed position while they drag a previously dropped, weighted scare line along the bottom to herd fish into the path of the net. Although these various types of active gear are not yet as common as those in Table 4.5, when used, they can cause considerable environmental damage, an issue I return to in Chapter 5.

In Palawan, increasingly efficient fishing gear as fine-meshed nets, baby trawls, and modified Danish seines have their origins in the Visayan Island region, where they developed as an adaptation to conditions of severe coastal resource depletion. Other types of active gear of Visayan origin include a kind of *lambat* (gill net) known as *kurantay,* an encircling gill net, and *talakop,* or ring net. As one Cuyonon fisherman told me, "We didn't know about those kinds of nets before." As successive waves of migrant Visayan fishermen arrived in San Vicente in search of better fishing, they brought these gear types with them, and as San Vicente's fish stocks have become depleted, some local fishermen have begun to turn to them as well.

Most fishermen spend 30 to 60 minutes to reach their initial fishing grounds but usually change locations several times during a single trip, depending on the fishing success they encounter along the way. The trips themselves last for many hours and may occur either during the day or at night, depending on the gear employed and the type of fish sought. Jigging for squid is a nighttime activity, whereas most hook-and-line fishing occurs during daylight hours. Setting nets may occur at any time. For a typical day trip, a boat leaves at daybreak and returns in the early afternoon; for a night trip, a boat leaves in the late afternoon and returns after sunrise the next day. Many night fishermen use kerosene lanterns to attract fish, and night fishing tends to be better during the new moon or the moon's first or last quarters. Moonlight distracts the fish from a fisherman's lantern light; when the moon is at or near full, night fishing is poor, and some fishermen do not go out at all.

How fishermen share the catch depends on ownership of the boat and net involved (see Figure 4.4). If the owner of the boat and net is not among the crew, he receives an agreed-upon share of the catch, usually one-fourth if the owner has provided the needed gasoline and oil, or one-sixth if the crew members choose to bear this expense. At the time of my research, gasoline sold locally for about U.S. $3.50 per gallon and was even more expensive in comparison with the typical cash incomes of fishing households shown in Table 4.3. If the owner of the net is different from the owner of the boat, then the net owner also receives a customary share of

Courtesy of James F. Eder

FIGURE 4.4 A fishing crew empties its nets

the catch. Once the owner of the boat and the net receive their share, all crew members equally divide among themselves the portion of the catch that remains. If a two-man crew includes the owner of the boat and net, the owner receives two payments, one as owner of the equipment and then for his labor. For example, a fisherman who owns his own boat and net receives half the catch for his capital investment, and then he and the crew member would split the remaining half. The crew member's share would be one-fourth of the total catch. Thus, the principle used in determining compensation is that capital comes before labor. In the Philippines, capital commands a considerable share of the total revenue.

After receiving his share, each crew member markets his own fish. Most hold back some fish for household consumption and sell the remainder to a fresh fish buyer, who represents the first step in a marketing chain that will deliver the fish to consumers in other locales. When fish are relatively abundant, fishermen bring their catch to one of the many local buying stations in San Vicente (see Figure 4.5), but when fish are scarce, buyers may crowd around newly returned fishing boats on the beach and compete for the catch (see Figure 4.6). Buyers dry most of their fish before leaving San Vicente to sell them in markets elsewhere. They immediately ship out the tastiest fish, known locally as "first class fish," on ice by bus or by truck to the Puerto Princesa City market.

People everywhere in the Philippines consume dried fish (*daing*) together with rice for breakfast. This breakfast is as common as bacon, eggs, and pancakes in the United States. Most Americans find the thought of eating dried fish unappetizing, especially when it comes to the head and the bones. I think of it as the marine equivalent of beef jerky, and I acquired quite a taste for it. When I am back in

Courtesy of James F. Eder

FIGURE 4.5   A fish-buying station in Alimanguan

Courtesy of James F. Eder

FIGURE 4.6   Fish buyers compete for a fisherman's catch

Courtesy of James F. Eder

FIGURE 4.7 A man prepares fish for drying

Arizona, dried fish is one of the foods in the Philippines that I most miss. People prepare dried fish by cleaning, filleting, and salting it and then laying it out to dry on racks in the sun. Fresh fish buyers do this processing on a large scale. Some may buy as much as 100 kilograms of fish in a single day and hire labor on a piecework basis as needed. If they have sufficient household labor and can wait to be paid for their catch, some fishermen prefer to dry their own fish and then sell it later to a dried fish buyer (see Figures 4.7 and 4.8). One of the most important fish for the dried fish trade in San Vicente is threadfin bream (*bisugo*). When I was last there, buyers paid U.S. $0.75 per kilogram for fresh threadfin bream and $2.10 per kilogram for dried bream. Fish loses about half its weight after drying, so the remainder of the difference between the two prices represents the return to the labor invested in the drying process.

The economic lives of fishing households are more complicated than this "catch it, dry it, and sell it" overview of the local fishing economy might suggest. The weather, seasonal variability in fish stocks, household labor supply, and market prices (among other factors) all influence on a daily basis the decisions that fishermen make regarding whether to fish, where to fish, and what fish to catch.

FIGURE 4.8 Fish put out to dry

Danny Decisions about fishing loom particularly large in the daily lives of poor fishermen such as Danelo, a specialist in fishing for squid and threadfin bream. Danelo, or Danny, owned only a small oar-powered *banca,* nylon line, and various hooks and jigs with which to fish. He and his wife Amelia migrated to San Vicente from Samar Island in 1988, immediately after their marriage, following in the path of Amelia's older brother and his family. Danny and Amelia had two children, both in school. Danny admitted that they had not prospered in San Vicente. His household income fell into the bottom third of Panindigan households in Table 4.3. He nonetheless prided himself on his fishing skills, which he considered superior to those of local Cuyonon residents who, he claimed, "don't really know how to fish."

When I asked Danny how his fishing techniques differed from those of Cuyonon farmers who similarly fish from small *bancas* with hook-and-line (implying that there was no difference), Danny became offended. He explained how he and other Visayan fishermen set several hooks at different depths from the same line, whereas Cuyonon fishermen only use one hook on a single line. He believed that his technique caught more fish because one could never be sure of the depth where fish were located or where they were biting. He also explained that Cuyonon fishermen paddle to a fishing spot, drop anchor, fish for a while, and then raise anchor and line and move on to another spot to repeat the process. In contrast, Visayan fishermen often do not drop anchor at all and instead let their boats drift slowly with the current. They do not need to repeatedly raise and lower their lines each time they move to a new location, and they catch more fish with their lines continuously in the water. I later asked several Cuyonon fishermen about Danny's explanation. They said that some Cuyonon fished by raising and lowering their nets as Danny described, but that others fished continuously in the same way as Danny, suggesting that Cuyonon and Visayan fishermen may not differ in their actual fishing techniques as much as some people say.

Danny estimated that he earned about U.S. $1.50 to 2.00 a night from squid and bream fishing, barely enough to support his family. During extended periods of fair weather, Danny fished every night, but during stormy weather or when the ocean was rough, Danny had to weigh the risks of venturing out. On several occasions, his small *banca* became swamped, twice in the surf near the beach and once out at sea. On days when such experiences threatened to repeat, he stayed home or sought a day job on land. He was once hired to help make cement hollow blocks at a local construction site. It was difficult and tedious work, he said, but "at least I got paid."

On the nights he went fishing, Danny had to choose between squid and bream fishing, which involve different equipment and different fishing locations. In making this choice, his main consideration was his ability to tolerate the risk of catching nothing at all. On the average, Danny made more money jigging for squid than fishing for bream, but the returns to bream fishing were relatively steady, whereas those to squid fishing were variable and unpredictable. Danny said he sometimes "hit the jackpot" with squid and pulled in hundreds of pesos, but on other nights, he came home empty-handed.

Another matter that had recently begun to figure in Danny's daily fishing decisions was whether to continue to ask his son, now 14 years old and in high school, to fish with him. Danny appreciated the help and the companionship, and his son was a willing crew member. But lately he had not been doing well in school because the fishing trips kept him from his homework, and on some days, he was too tired to attend school at all. Danny and Amelia acknowledged that they could not afford to send their son to college, but they at least wanted him to graduate from high school. Neither Danny nor Amelia had attended high school, and it was an obvious point of pride that their own children might at least get that far in life.

Rolito   Rolito and Eriberta, also from the Visayan Islands (Rolito is from Cebu, Eriberta from Leyte), are better off than Danny and Amelia. Their household income placed them comfortably in the middle third of Panindigan households shown in Table 4.3. They had five children, four in school and one recently graduated from high school. Rolito owned two pumpboats, an older one with a 3 horsepower engine and a newer one with a 10 horsepower engine. He also owned two fishing nets, one made of nylon intended for smaller, schooling fish and another made of cotton, larger in mesh, intended for jack, tuna, and other large "first class" fish. Rolito used the larger boat with the assistance of two regular crew members. After deducting all expenses and crew shares, he estimated that he averaged U.S. $4.00 to 6.00 a night, a figure he described to me as his "take home pay." Eriberta dried fish for a marine products company and earned an average of $1.00 to 1.20 per day. Lately, their oldest son had been using their smaller boat to fish with a friend once or twice a week, to earn money to meet personal expenses. According to Eriberta, their son was preoccupied with his girlfriend and was "not really serious about fishing," but as he still lived at home, the family welcomed his occasional contributions of fish and money.

Among Rolito's daily decisions were what fish to catch and which of his nets to use. To make this decision he relied on the advice of his crew members and the reports of other fishermen regarding their own recent experience. When fishing was good close by, Rolito used the nylon net and visited a favorite reef several kilometers immediately offshore. Otherwise, he brought the cotton net and several Styrofoam ice chests and set out in search of larger fish many hours away. Rolito and his crew were sometimes away for two days at a time, traveling far south on Palawan to fish in isolated waters off sparsely populated stretches of Palawan's west coast. Rolito told me that he and his crew had once fished in this way "all the way to Borneo," mainly for the adventure of it, traveling about 15 hours in each direction. I disbelieved this story when I first heard it, but I subsequently learned that fishermen from Palawan, even from as far north as San Vicente, periodically enter Malaysian territorial waters. On these longer fishing trips, Rolito and his crew brought along enough ice to keep their catch fresh until they returned. Although such expeditions carried risks, including the possibility of mechanical breakdown far from home, they were almost always successful. Rolito estimates that the net revenue (minus expenses) from his share of the catch from these longer trips was about U.S. $16 to 20. From the perspective of most fishermen, the main disadvantage of Rolito's long fishing trips was their considerable upfront cost, particularly for the large amounts of gasoline needed for refueling along the way. Most fishermen could not afford the necessary advance purchases of food and gasoline for such trips, nor could their families easily meet daily expenses in their absence. Rolito's ability to periodically undertake extended fishing trips shows that he was relatively well off compared with his neighbors.

I came to know both Danny and Rolito pretty well, and I was struck how they differed in their economic security and self-confidence. Danny was beset by worries about what best to do next and lived, in his own words, "one scratch, one peck," a wry local reference to how chickens eat. Rolito, though not rich, lived comfortably by local standards, and he had found a fishing strategy that worked well for him. I had difficulty getting him to talk about the fishing-related decisions he made as he went about his daily life. In his view, he was "already established" and could just "play out his hand" (Rolito played cards in his spare time). By this, he meant that he would continue to do what he was doing because it had been working reasonably well. "This is where I am in life," Rolito told me, "I won't be going any further." His main concern was that his children would do better in life than he and Eriberta.

Farming

Although farming and fishing coexist side-by-side in the coastal zone, they have different ecologies and call for a different style of fieldwork. Fishing households tend to be aggregated in clusters of various sizes along the beach front, whereas farming households tend to be scattered, and the more so their farms. I often met and interviewed farmers individually, whereas I typically encountered fishermen in small groups. Lacking a handy means to call ahead, I sometimes arrived at the house of a farmer and found him gone, but if the farmer was in his field, I could always attempt to track him down there. I impressed more than one farmer with my willingness to navigate a steep hillside or a maze of narrow rice paddy bunds (the narrow "dikes" that separate paddies of slightly different elevation) to ask my questions, as perplexing or unnecessary as these may have seemed. However, if I arrived at the house of fisherman when he was away fishing, I was pretty much out of luck and had to return on another day.

The questions I asked of farmers were also different from those I asked of fishermen. Farmers have different kinds of productive assets. They own agricultural land and farm animals, rather than the boats, motors, and nets owned by fishermen (Table 4.1). Farmers earn their incomes from different productive activities, and they receive their incomes on a variable schedule. Fishing households characteristically receive cash incomes on a daily basis. Granted, daily incomes vary, depending on the weather and the catch, but the heads of most fishing households easily estimated their average daily income by combining the husband's typical share of fishing revenue with the wife's income, if any, from making dried fish. Farming incomes are much less regular because they are based on postharvest sales of rice, corn, and tree crops, and on periodic sale of farm animals. To estimate income from agricultural activities, I had to reconstruct a farmer's sale of farm produce during an entire year. Farmers also have different labor requirements and a different sexual division of labor. Women rarely go out to sea with men to fish, but they engage in a variety of agricultural activities, in addition to their work in the home. Looking at a more personal side of fieldwork, I found that visiting farms was a welcome respite from visiting the beach. Despite the beauty of the seashore, there was monotony about it and the heat and sand fleas could be brutal. Farms were cooler, and there was always something new to see.

On the coastal plain where irrigated rice cultivation prevails, fields are laid out checkerboard style. Irrigation canals originate from water sources in the foothills to supply the fields. Here and there, feeder roads head off in either direction from the highway toward farmhouses and small settlements. Farm plots are typically 1 or 2 hectares in size, and farmers grow one, two, or even three crops of rice annually, depending on the variety of the rice and the reliability of the water supply. Irrigated rice farmers in San Vicente employ water buffalo to draw plows and harrows in preparing their fields, and they make extensive use of chemical fertilizers and pesticides. Not all of the plain is irrigated or suitable for rice cultivation. Coconut palms, banana plants, and mango and cashew trees grow on the coastal plain as well (see Figure 4.9). On the hillsides, farms are irregular in shape and size and most can be reached only by trail. Here farmers clear their fields annually. The fields are entirely rain-fed, mostly planted in corn, sweet potato, and cassava. Many upland farmers also have large stands of banana plants and mango, cashew, citrus, and other fruit trees. On all farms, pigs and chickens are the most common farm animals; some farmers also raise goats, and the more prosperous ones keep cows (see Figure 4.10).

FIGURE 4.9   A lowland farm at New Canipo

FIGURE 4.10   An upland farm near Port Barton

The most significant environmental impact of smallholder farming in tropical regions like Palawan is the loss of the biodiversity that results when settlers remove forest cover to establish their farms. On the coastal plain where farmers manage irrigated rice fields, relatively stable ecological conditions reemerge. The main environmental effects of farming concern the use of agricultural chemicals, but no studies exist to demonstrate the environmental affects of these applications in San Vicente. On upland farms, ecological conditions are less stable on hillside plots left fallow or planted in annual crops such as rice or corn. These hillsides are vulnerable to soil degradation and erosion. A hillside farm fully planted in tree crops more closely resembles the original land cover, and relative environmental stability returns. Few upland farmers use agricultural chemicals except for very specific purposes, such as to induce flowering on mango trees.

The concerns of individual farmers, like those of fishermen, vary depending on the weather, the market, and their own particular circumstances. Following are some examples of the kinds of decisions farmers must make in the course of their everyday lives in San Vicente.

Edward   I met Edward quite by accident. Upon losing my way one day, I approached a farmhouse to ask directions and was attacked by guard geese! I had never been chased by geese, and I was glad that no one was watching. After hearing the racket, Edward came running from his field to rescue me. We laughed about it—geese are easier to take care of than dogs, he explained, and more reliable—and I had made a new friend. Edward was from Taytay, where he had previously been involved with a local politician in a rattan-collecting enterprise that lacked the necessary permits. The authorities apprehended and fined them, and Edward decided to move on. He never received any inheritance because his father was given to drinking and squandered his family's wealth. When Edward arrived in San Vicente 10 years earlier, he did not have "a peso in his pocket." Edward ever since has been a tenant farmer on 3 hectares of irrigated rice land owned by his *compadre,* the baptismal sponsor or godparent of one of his children. Edward benefited from the proximity of his rice paddies to a municipal irrigation system, and he planted two and sometimes three crops of rice a year. After deducting the costs of fertilizer and pesticide, he gave one-third of every harvest to the owner and kept the remaining two-thirds for himself. He also received income from the sale of farm animals and from coconuts, bananas, and fruits grown on a nearby hillside, but most of his income was from the sale of rice.

Edward was married and had five children, but he described himself as a "single farmer." All his children were in school, and his wife Gloria was largely confined to their house by the demands of childcare and ill health. Edward's primary concern was how to develop a second income source to help pay for the college educations of at least some of his children. As it stood, the family was barely getting by, and Edward was constantly in debt. He did not appear to sell rice so much as to use it to pay back loans taken out to meet consumption, education, and healthcare expenses. According to Edward, farming alone is not enough to support a family in today's world; you also need a "business" (*negocio*), so that you can accumulate capital and savings. Gloria had long wanted to open a small store adjacent to their house, but they never had sufficient money to buy the initial stock of goods.

Rosalier   Rosalier was in a better resource position than Edward. He had recently acquired almost 2 hectares of land after the previous owner, his nephew, defaulted on a loan using the land as collateral. One hectare contained coconuts and the remainder was suitable for irrigated rice cultivation but lacked access to a reliable water supply. Rosalier needed to develop a local water source and finish constructing his fields. He and his wife Rosela married late, and until their first child arrived, she regularly helped in the field. Before they acquired their own land, they relied mainly on upland farming on a hillside that Rosela's mother had originally cleared and planted.

Like Edward, Rosalier lived in Alimanguan, but comparing their respective household incomes with those of the New Agutaya farming households shown in Table 4.3, Edward's household fell in the bottom third, and Rosalier's household fell in the middle third. Rosalier and Rosela were not locked into the same credit-debt trap as Edward and Gloria, but they did not seem very prosperous for all their projects and for the length of time that Rosalier had lived in San Vicente (he arrived in 1960 but only married Rosela in 2002). His was a history of missed opportunities. In the 1960s, good farm land was still available for homesteading in San Vicente or could be purchased for very little, but Rosalier never acquired any. His father owned a farm along the beach, which he later subdivided among his children, but Rosalier sold his share early, before the value of beachfront property skyrocketed. Rosalier also claimed that he had been cheated on this and other past economic transactions. Rosela's sister told me that Rosalier was hard-working but that he "needed a manager" to direct his labor in more productive directions and that he did not know how to plan for the future. Relatives of Rosalier and Rosela arranged their late marriage to help get Rosalier's life back on track. Others mentioned that Rosalier's pride at having finally acquired rice land of his own had clouded his judgment regarding its potential. They believed the water source that he was stubbornly attempting to develop was at best adequate for only one crop of rice a year, and that he would do better to develop the upland farm that his wife had inherited from her mother by planting mangoes and other fruit trees. Both Edward and Rosalier have had their share of bad luck. The difference is that Edward was largely a victim of poverty and other material circumstances, including an ill wife and a large family, whereas Rosalier's current lot in life was due mainly to his own poor decisions.

Teodoro   Both Edward and Rosalier were of Visayan origin, and each was comfortable with the style of irrigated rice farming that predominates on San Vicente's coastal plain. Rosalier chose not to develop an upland farm; others did just that successfully. Teodoro, a Cuyonon from New Canipo, was 7 years old when he arrived in Palawan in 1962. His mother and father were among the earliest Cuyonon settlers in San Vicente described in Chapter 2. As a boy and later as a young man, Teodoro helped his father clear the forest from his New Canipo homestead, and together with his wife Susana, Teodoro operated a 7-hectare upland farm that represented his inherited share of that homestead. Their farm was located on a hillside, bounded on the lower edge by an irrigated rice farm on the coastal plain and on the upper edge by the forest boundary. Five hectares were planted in coconut, banana, cashew, avocado, citrus, and other fruit trees. Teodoro and Susana maintained the remaining 2 hectares as a fallow reserve for the annual cultivation of corn and upland rice. They also keep one water buffalo, several cows and pigs, and about thirty chickens. Their large, varied, and well-maintained farm had made Teodoro and Susana prosperous by local standards, but in an old-fashioned, self-sufficient way. "We have lots of food but no money," was how Susana characterized their circumstances to me.

Teodoro and Susana's principal concern was their distance to the market. They lived so far away that even the act of selling a pig took most of a day. Teodoro first brought the pig by a buffalo-drawn sled to the beach and then loaded it on a boat for a 45-minute trip to the nearest hog buyer in Alimanguan. Concerns about money had recently become more urgent because their youngest daughter was excelling in high school and hoped to attend college in Puerto Princesa City. The relative remoteness of their farm made it difficult for Teodoro and Susana to decide how best to increase their cash income. They knew that some farmers in San Vicente had done well by replacing their "native" hogs with improved, hybrid varieties that gain weight faster, but they were unsure if they could meet the more stringent care and feeding requirements or secure the immunizations needed to prevent illness or wasting. Another possibility they were considering was to plant their remaining fallow land in calamondin orange, a common Philippine citrus. The small fruits commanded a high price in Puerto Princesa City, and Teodoro recognized the environmental benefits of having his hillsides entirely planted in tree crops rather than leaving some areas exposed to the elements and vulnerable to erosion. However, citrus fruit is perishable and they worried that they might be unable to deliver ripe fruit to market in a timely fashion. Also, once their land was fully planted in trees, they would be unable to grow their own rice and would instead have to buy it, a prospect they both found unsettling. When I was last in San Vicente, Teodoro and Susana were still considering these and other possibilities.

Supplementary Economic Activities

One of the most widely heard pieces of local economic wisdom in San Vicente is that "you cannot do just one thing in life and expect to get by," because a single income or a single occupation is just not enough to make household ends meet. I showed how one of Edward's problems was that neither he nor his wife had yet found a secondary economic activity to supplement his income from farming. Fishing or farming may be the primary occupations of most individuals, and many households, like Edward's, rely exclusively on income from one or the other, but in many other households income from a second or even a third source supplements income from fishing and farming.

As different as fishing and farming may sound, in many San Vicente households, one activity supplements the other. Fishing is supplementary to farming in the numerous Cuyonon and Agutaynen households where people primarily farm for a living. One or more members of such households characteristically fish "on the side," often for recreation as well as for subsistence. In the largely Cuyonon community of New Canipo, for example, the primary livelihood is rain-fed rice farming and cultivation of coconuts, cashew, and other tree crops. In the largely Agutaynen community of New Agutaya, water resources are more developed and the principal household income source is twice-yearly irrigated rice cultivation. In many households in both communities, an adult male goes out to sea several nights a week in a small, nonmotorized outrigger to fish with a hook and line, with the catch intended primarily for household consumption and secondarily for sale to neighbors. Fishing by Cuyonon and Agutaynen farmers has only a modest environmental impact in comparison with the market-oriented fishing of their Visayan neighbors. As one Cuyonon farmer put it to me, "Once I've caught enough fish for dinner or for breakfast, I return to shore, because I still have work to do on the farm."

The reverse situation obtains in many Visayan households in Alimanguan whose members supplement their fishing incomes with seasonal farm work. Here, Palawan's distinctive west coast weather pattern becomes important. During the northeast monsoon from January to May, the ocean is largely calm on this side of Palawan, and fishermen face few problems with the weather. San Vicente's important squid-fishing season falls during this period of relative ocean calm. But the southwest monsoon, from June to December, brings large waves and periodic storms to Palawan's west coast, and on many days fishermen curtail their fishing trips or do not venture out at all. Some fishing households in San Vicente continue to fish all year and settle for reduced income during the southwest monsoon, whereas many others during this period seek supplementary income in the agricultural economy, a choice that reduces temporarily exploitative pressures on fish stocks.

Social class position is an important determinant of how fishing households earn supplementary incomes from farming activities. Some of the more prosperous fishing households have purchased farmland, and there they plant and harvest one crop of rice each year on fields seasonally inundated by the southwest monsoon rains. Most people who alternate fishing and farming, however, including many residents of the community of Alimanguan, are poorer. They lack farmland of their own and instead work in the fields of others in return for a share of the harvest. Danelo and Amelia, the co-heads of one of the fishing households described earlier, annually supplemented their fishing income by share harvesting. Three-fourths of all the rice they harvested each day went to the owner of the field, and they kept one-fourth for themselves. (Share harvesting agreements vary with the labor supply; when labor is scarce, field owners may offer as much as a third of the harvest to prospective harvesters.) Danny and Amelia did not sell the rice they harvested; they instead saved it for future consumption. They estimated that with about a month of hard work during the harvest season, they accumulated enough rice to feed their household for about 4 months of the year. After that, Amelia said, "we go back to buying it."

In New Agutaya, which lies along a stretch of the coast popular with beach seiners, fishing and farming are mutually supplementary in yet another way.

I recounted in Chapter 1 my own first experience with beach seining and explained how coastal resource managers view seining as environmentally damaging. Beach seines are fine-meshed nets ranging in length from 500 meters to 1,500 meters or more, set by men in outriggers who attempt to encircle a school of fish or shrimp in a shallow part of the ocean near the beach. Each end or "wing" of the net consists of a pull rope that is then brought ashore, such that the net forms a large "U" and the two pull ropes are separated by a distance of several hundred meters on the beach. Two teams of eight or more net pullers, mostly women and children, haul the net to shore, one team at each wing of the net (see Figure 1.1).

Beach seines catch everything in their path, including small fish and fish not consumed by humans. They are another example of the active and highly efficient fishing gears I discussed earlier. However, for those who practice beach seining, there is nothing wrong with it and nothing is wasted. Seiners dry any fish not considered edible and ground them into fish meal to feed to pigs. Some New Agutaya women whose husbands are full-time farmers regularly participate in beach seining as net pullers, intending not just to put food on their family's table but to also to help feed their pigs. Fish meal is a high-quality pig feed and a nutritionally desirable supplement to the rice bran, cassava, plantain, and other plant foods that compose the bulk of the pig feed on most San Vicente farms. Worldwide, fishmeal is a critically important feed ingredient in aquaculture production (e.g., salmon, trout, and shrimp) as well as in hog and poultry production, and growing demand for fishmeal for these purposes may increase stress on the world's fisheries and undermine the sustainability of aquaculture systems (Kristofersson and Anderson 2006).

In many other San Vicente households, income from fishing or farming is supplemented by still other economic activities, collectively known as "sidelines." These supplementary economic activities, like beach seining, are often the pursuits of woman in combination with their housekeeping and childrearing responsibilities. Ownership of a small store (and many stores are very small) is the most frequent sideline, but secondary occupations vary widely. In San Vicente, they include making and selling roof thatch or cooked food, providing preschool day care, or serving as a pastor or an Avon cosmetics dealer. Excluded from my discussion here are people such as schoolteachers, salaried employees of the municipal government, and individuals engaged full-time in business enterprises. Such people are not necessarily "big people." They may be consumers of coastal resources, but they are not themselves directly engaged in resource exploitation.

The use of such terms as *secondary occupation* or *sideline* referring to such activities does not do justice to their economic significance in household economic life. *Occupational multiplicity,* as I formally term this phenomenon, often is crucial to household survival. A woman may only have said "it's just my sideline" in response to a query from me or my research assistant about a supplementary economic activity, but left unspoken that it keeps food on her family's table or enables the family to send a child to high school. Further, in a changing economic world, older economic activities are closing off even as new ones are constantly appearing, and today's sideline may become tomorrow's principal income source. Here is how two households have made supplementary income-earning activities part of their household economic strategies.

Remy   Remedios or Remy, the sister of Teodoro, whose upland farm in New Canipo I described earlier, long worked on a neighboring upland farm together with her own husband, Ramon, and their four children. New Canipo has an elementary school but not a high school, and when their children began attending high school in a neighboring community, the one-hour walk each way meant that they were no longer able to return home at mid-day for lunch. Remy drew on produce from their farm to prepare various snack foods for the children to consume at school, such as boiled plantains, deep-fried and sugared sweet potato slices, and glutinous rice cooked in coconut milk and wrapped in banana leaf. Other students living at a similar distance from the high school, but on lowland farms specializing in irrigated rice, inquired if those same snacks might be offered for sale, and Remy's sideline was born. She began to travel to the high school at the noon hour bringing baskets of snack foods for sale to students during their lunch break.

Ramon and Remy, like Teodoro and Susana, spoke with me regarding the hardships of living in the foothills, away from the coastal plain. They seldom ate fresh fish because it was too time-consuming to walk to the beach to look for someone selling it, and the 30-minute walk to the New Canipo elementary school was hard on the children, especially in the rainy season. Upland living had its advantages including agricultural goods that many fishing and farming households on the coastal plain lacked, and Remy added substantial value to those goods before sale. Remy and Ramon did not keep records, but they estimated that about 20 percent of their total annual cash income derived from Remy's "sideline."

Anecia   Anecia lived in Port Barton with her husband Efren and their four children. This family was Visayan, and they long relied entirely on Efren's income from fishing to support the household. Recently Efren's declining fishing income had prompted Anecia to begin work at a nearby beach resort, cleaning rooms and helping in the kitchen. She felt that the pay, about U.S. $2.50 per day, was poor, but she liked working there because it got her out of the house and she enjoyed the company of the other women employed at the resort. Her main concern was improper supervision of her children, because her work schedule was irregular and her employer sometimes asked her on short notice to work into the evening when Efren was away fishing. Anecia was particularly concerned about the well-being of her teenaged daughter, who had recently acquired a boyfriend. Anecia did not feel that in their present economic circumstances she could quit her job and stay at home. Anecia and Efren estimated that her earnings currently account for about a third of their total cash income, and they emphasized that on days when Efren was sick or the weather was bad, Anecia's earnings were their only income.

I find it difficult to generalize completely about the environmental impacts of supplementary economic activities. Some, like beach seining, may be environmentally damaging. Others, like Remy's snack-making sideline and Anecia's job at the beach resort, seemed environmentally neutral. For the most part, the supplementary economic activities I observed in San Vicente did not appear to increase direct pressure on natural resources.

COPING WITH CHANGE

In the remainder of this chapter, I show how individuals and households in San Vicente attempt to cope with resource depletion and other challenges to their economic well-being posed by global forces. One piece of local wisdom is that households must have more than one thing going for them to survive in the present world; another piece is that the world is always changing, and so too must household economic strategies if people are not to be left behind. "Steady as she goes," as one fisherman expressed it to me, just does not work anymore.

The Rising Price of Gasoline

The most immediate coping challenge that most fishing-dependent households face arises from rising gasoline prices on one hand and declining fish stocks on the other. Almost everyone is feeling the "squeeze" (this English term is widely used locally) and looking for ways to adapt. I first met Bruce Lee when I observed him delivering freshly caught fish to a fish buyer on the beach, and I hung around to talk about his boat afterward. (Yes, that really is his first name; his father was a fan of Bruce Lee movies). Bruce Lee was from Samar, one of the Visayan Islands, but he had lived in San Vicente for about 15 years. He had recently repainted his boat and installed a new 10 horsepower engine. Bruce Lee used this boat to fish with his net for several years on a regular basis, and we eventually took several trips in it together. When I saw him most recently, however, he was using a different and smaller boat. Bruce Lee explained that declining fish catches and the rising price of gasoline were the cause of too many failed fishing trips when he had not caught enough fish even to cover his fuel costs, much less to earn money or bring home fish to feed his family. He had decided instead to borrow a smaller boat, with a more economical 5 horsepower engine, and fish for threadfin bream with a hook and line. The boat was owned by the fish buyer to whom Bruce Lee normally sold his catch, and as rent for the boat, the buyer received one-sixth of the catch. Bruce Lee reasoned that even though he had to part with a portion of his catch, his smaller fuel costs meant that he came out ahead.

Bruce Lee's cousin Jose also spoke of being squeezed between rising fuel costs and declining catches; he estimated that when he first arrived in San Vicente in 1990, he caught about 20 kilograms of fish every night, but his nightly catch was now only 10 kilograms. Jose coped with his declining catch not by switching to a smaller boat, but by cutting back on the number of his fishing trips while making each trip longer in duration. He was accustomed to going out to fish almost every night, and this new routine required more careful household budgeting to cover the days when he had no fish to sell. He was also considering reducing his crew size. Jose normally fished and shared his catch with his brother-in-law and his son-in-law. Neither had a boat or net of their own, and Jose wanted to help them economically, "because they also have families to support." Otherwise, he said that he could make do with just one of them helping. If gasoline prices continued to rise, Jose told me, he could not "afford to be so generous" and he would reluctantly have to tell his brother-in-law that he could no longer be a member of the crew.

Both Bruce Lee and Jose made fairly conservative responses to the coping challenges posed by resource depletion. They each stuck with what they knew best, fishing, and modified their fishing strategies in the hope that fishing would remain profitable for them. Other men and women, however, previously engaged in fishing or farming, turn to entirely new kinds of activities in an attempt to survive—and hopefully, to prosper—in the face of global changes. For the Philippines as a whole, probably the best known coping response of this kind is overseas contract work. Millions of Filipinos, mostly of rural origin, today work in a variety of occupations in the Middle East, Singapore, Hong Kong, and elsewhere. Here, I describe additional local responses to the challenges and opportunities posed by global change, responses from men and women whose resourcefulness and willingness to experiment continued to surprise and impress me throughout my fieldwork.

Silkworms, Monitor Lizards, and Tourist Guides

One day I was returning by boat from fieldwork in a distant community. The boatman reminded me that I had intended to put ashore at a second community on the way back, to look up the president of the local women's association regarding supplementary livelihood activities that her group might be sponsoring. I was tired and out of sorts (my interviews that morning had not yielded much new information), and I was inclined to forget about the second stop, reasoning that I already knew what I was likely to see or hear there as well. Nonetheless, we ended up stopping anyway. The boatman wanted to visit with a cousin about a business matter, and so I went ahead and looked up Edna, whose name had been previously given to me by a relative in another community. Upon arriving at her house, I saw cardboard boxes everywhere, as if Edna and her family might be in the process of moving in or out. Of course, I had to ask what was in the boxes, and just when I thought I had seen it all, I saw silkworms—hundreds of them!

I had never seen silkworms in my life, and I certainly was not expecting to see any in San Vicente, but there they were. I learned that the wife of the previous mayor had sponsored a silkworm-raising project for local women and, with the support of the municipal government, she had arranged for the marketing and weaving of the raw silk produced by local women. Edna was the local organizer of the project, but when the sponsor's husband suffered defeat in his bid for re-election, the new mayor withdrew municipal support for the project. However, Edna had gamely continued on, hoping to make a go of it. She had a buyer lined up in Puerto Princesa City for her product, but she was encountering difficulty finding suitable local plants to feed her caterpillars and was not sure if she would continue. Nonetheless, I was impressed. Several months later, I saw raw silk scarves of local manufacture for sale in one of the souvenir shops in Puerto Princesa City, but I was unable to determine their origin.

Local resourcefulness and imagination in the face of the new opportunities posed by global change sometimes outruns reality and even common sense, and some would-be sidelines never really get off the ground. Nicanor, the young son-in-law of Teodoro and Susana in New Canipo, was also an upland farmer but he hoped for something better and "more modern" in life than farming. I met up with him after he had learned that a Chinese merchant in Puerto Princesa City was seeking live monitor lizards and other native wildlife to re-sell as pets to overseas buyers. Monitor lizards in Palawan are not endangered, nor do they enjoy special protected status, but the provincial government bans export of native wildlife, and the merchant's participation in the international wildlife trade was clandestine. Locally, monitor lizards are considered pests, particularly on farms. The adult lizards can reach four feet in length and sometimes attack and eat chickens. Some upland farmers trap and even eat the lizards. Nicanor reasoned that he could earn good money by trapping and selling what appeared to be an endless supply of monitor lizards in New Canipo. He eventually caught about twenty-five lizards, but after making several money-losing trips to Puerto Princesa City, where he received less money for the lizards and spent more on transportation and other expenses than he had planned, he became discouraged and gave up. He described his project to me later as a failure. He still hoped to be something more than a farmer, but farming for now was what he had to do, because at least "you can count on it."

Other San Vicente residents have yet-to-be actualized plans for doing side-line work. Efren, the husband of Anecia who worked at the beach resort, aspired to be a part-time tourist guide. Gregarious in nature, encouraged by his wife's relatively steady income from the resort, and discouraged by his own declining fish catch, he reasoned that he could make better money by hiring out himself and his boat to take tourists on day trips for swimming or snorkeling, even if only for a few days each week. His main problem was meeting potential customers—I was his first—because his English skills are limited and his small boat lacks an awning to shelter passengers from sun and rain. Efren hoped that Anecia could refer potential customers to him, but all of the resorts already had contracted "boatmen" whom they recommended to guests. Anecia feared that she would get in trouble with her manager if she referred any guests to Efren. For my part, I hired Efren and his boat twice, and I much enjoyed and learned from his company. During one trip, his boat broke down, and I had to help paddle it to a deserted island where we were stuck for hours before we finally returned home. During the next trip, we were caught in a squall and returned home cold and soaking wet. Nonetheless, I thoroughly enjoyed both trips and I very much look forward to seeing and traveling again with Efren when I am next back in San Vicente, although I still fear that his business skills and equipment will not prove attractive to many tourists!

How Gender Matters

Although it is difficult to earn a living in San Vicente today by fishing or farming and even to find a good sideline to supplement that living, some people really do get ahead in life. I do not mean to suggest that they become rich, but neither do all households live hand to mouth; many accumulate modest savings to cover unexpected expenses or to invest in ways that promise to improve household economic well-being. Edna may have raised silkworms by herself, and Nicanor may have trapped monitor lizards by himself, but each was a member of a household where other members contributed in different ways to the household's pool of labor and financial resources. Once I got to know people, I often asked about their plans for the future and, specifically, about how they might use potential savings to purchase new equipment or make strategic economic investments. I thought it was too nosy to ask about anyone's actual savings, and most people would not have told me anyway, so I posed the question in hypothetical terms. During such questioning, I found that husbands and wives did not always agree regarding what to do next, and I eventually became quite interested in the role of gender in decisions about household economic plans (see Eder 2006).

Among the beach seine pullers I met during my first day on the beach was Elisa, a lively and outspoken woman who seemed like she might be a good informant. I subsequently visited her and her husband Reynaldo at their house, and during several visits, I got to know them very well. They were both from Mindoro Island, near Luzon, and had a difficult start in San Vicente. They had traveled to Palawan by boat, following another boat bearing Reynaldo's brother and his wife, who drowned when their boat sank in a storm. Reynaldo began life in San Vicente as a farmer, but after finding it difficult and unprofitable, he decided to try his luck at fishing. For the first several years, he borrowed a small outrigger from a neighbor and eventually purchased in succession a boat of his own, an engine, and a net. Elisa worked regularly as a seine puller and became quite knowledgeable about beach seining (it is not as simple as it might look in Figure 1.1!). In this household, the wife supplemented the fishing income of her husband with income of her own. As a result, Reynaldo and Elisa had saved money, but they had different ideas about how to use it, a disagreement I discovered only after interviewing them separately about the matter.

Reynaldo hoped to buy an additional 500 meters of the same type of net he already employed to increase his potential catch. He noted that the high cost of gasoline made it more important than ever to "maximize" (his word) his catch during each fishing trip, and a bigger net meant a bigger catch. Elisa also hoped to buy a net, but of the type used for beach seining. She reasoned that because the owners of beach seines receive 50 percent of the catch, while all the pullers divided the other 50 percent among themselves, she would receive a much greater income from beach seining as a net owner than as a net puller. She stated that she could quickly recover the cost of the net and then some. She estimated that the total catch from an episode of beach seining could be as high as U.S. $24.00 worth of fish. As a net owner, her share would then be worth $12.00, but as a net puller along with eleven other pullers, her share would only be worth $1.00. Reynaldo and Elisa both asked themselves the same question, "What new gear can we purchase that would enable me to make a greater contribution to household income?" Their divergent answers reflect their different skills and positions in the household. Each could justify purchasing a particular kind of net based on the benefits that would accrue to the household as seen from their position within it. While Reynaldo and Elisa were not, to my knowledge, quarreling about making this decision, it was something that they would need to resolve.

In another household similarly dependent entirely on fishing, discussions between husband and wife about what to do next took a different turn. Alfred and Alma, both from Samar Island in the Visayas, wanted to market Alfred's catch more profitably. Alfred operates a fish corral and specializes in catching rabbitfish (*danggit*), and together they had been drying his catch and selling it locally. Dried rabbitfish commands a much higher price in Manila where urban consumers prize it for its flavor and long shelf life. Alma proposed to use their current savings to buy large quantities of dried rabbitfish locally, combine it with the rabbitfish dried from their own catch, and take the entire lot to Manila for sale. Alfred opposed her plan, believing that she would never recover her expenses and that, having never been to Manila, she would probably (among other things) become lost.

The issue was decided when Alma, over Alfred's objections, made a sudden trip to Manila with twelve large boxes of dried fish, a trip she described to me as a "trial run" and which Alfred described as "doomed to failure." Alma returned the following week. She had stayed with a helpful cousin whom she had not seen in years. After deducting all her expenses, she turned a tidy profit. I learned later from Alma's sister Rose that when Alma later prepared to make a second trip to Manila, Alfred declared his desire to participate in the venture as well, "in case she needed help," a change-of-mind that Rose found amusing. This case shows that husbands and wives, as co-heads of households, might have different ideas about what fishing gear to buy next, as did Reynaldo and Elisa, and they might differ in their willingness to take risks. Alma clearly felt that the potential payoff from her proposed venture was worth the risks; initially Alfred did not. I learned of other such cases where wives were more willing than husbands to try something new and to take risks in the interest of improving household economic well-being. The willingness of women to take risks seems to be an attribute of gender roles in the rural Philippines (Eder 2006).

Change Is Continuous

Not all household efforts to cope with change hinge on a single decision or a specific date or event, such as Alma's trip to Manila. As several other cases demonstrate, coping with change is an ongoing process, and new household economic strategies may emerge gradually and in relatively uncalculated fashion. Lando long fished for a living, and his wife Gina was busy raising their small children. He sold his fish live to a local fish buyer. Once the children were in elementary school, however, Gina began to make dried fish out of some of Lando's catch to supplement their household income with a larger return expected from the sale of dried fish. Later, their oldest daughter began to help with fish-drying after school, and Gina began to employ the daughters of neighbors on a piece-work basis as well. Before long, they ceased selling any fresh fish at all, and Gina began to buy fresh fish from nearby fishermen to expand the drying operation. Eventually, Lando and Gina became full-time fresh fish buyers and dried-fish makers. Although Lando still went fishing occasionally, on most days he loaned out his boat to other fishermen in return for a share of their catch. His work mainly consisted of delivering the dried fish that Gina produced to fish buyers. He hoped to buy a motorcycle and use it to transport dried fish to the town of Roxas (see Figure 2.1), where it would command a higher price.

Like Lando, Peter had fished for a living for a long time, but his wife Rachel had different skills and interests than Gina did. Rachel operated a small store and had a knack for *negocio* (business), but she also liked going to sea. When Peter tired of fishing, they began making occasional trips together to Binga, the northernmost community in San Vicente and one accessible only by a two-hour boat ride. They brought along rice and other commodities to trade locally for dried fish to sell in their home community and commercial center of Aliman-guan. As these "barter trade" trips proved economically successful, Peter eventually stopped fishing entirely, Rachel closed her store, and they began making three or four such trips a week. As in the case of Lando and Gina, what had begun as a sideline for Peter and Rachel evolved into a full-time business that yielded a higher income than they had previously earned separately. Neither wished to disclose to me their actual income, but Rachel suggested that with their new enterprise, they were earning about 50 percent more than they had before.

Coping is Not Easy

Evolving into new occupations does not come easily. Sidelines may lead to something bigger and better, as I showed with these last two cases, but they are not without risks and can easily turn problematic or sour, as with the silkworm-raising and monitor-lizard trapping projects described earlier. Bruce Lee's wife Russielle recounted to me how in years past, she supplemented their household income by buying and selling clothes, at a time when none were sold locally. She took orders from neighbors for various clothing items; when she had enough orders to justify a trip, she traveled to Roxas by bus and bought the items there, marking up the price upon her return to recover her expenses and make a profit. Eventually their community grew large enough that someone opened a dry goods store, and Russielle no longer could attract customers to her buy-and-sell enterprise. An energetic and determined woman, Russielle then turned to hog-raising, but her very success at it made her and Bruce Lee concerned about the increasing costs of the needed feed. As I showed earlier, Bruce Lee grew discouraged about the profitability of fishing and began to cultivate sweet potato and manioc on a part-time basis to help feed their pigs. When I last saw Bruce Lee, he joked that when I next returned to San Vicente, he might already be a farmer!

Russielle and Bruce Lee successfully replaced one sideline with another, but for others, change is more difficult. Everything seemed to be going well with Peter and Rachel's barter-trade business until the construction of a road from Taytay to Binga, the fishing community they served by boat. With the opening of the road, trucks brought in trade goods more cheaply and in greater quantity, and several local stores opened. Local fishermen took their dried fish to the new stores, and Peter and Rachel's barter trade enterprise collapsed. Conceivably, they could have found something else to do locally, as Russielle did when her own buy-and-sell operation faced new competition, but Peter and Rachel wanted to stick with what they knew best. When I last saw her, Rachel was in tears. Two of their children were in college in Puerto Princesa City unable to meet their tuition payments. Peter and Rachel were preparing to sell their house in Alimanguan and move to a more isolated place on the east coast of Palawan where there are many small islands that "will never have roads built to them." In such a place, they hoped to begin again with their way of making a living and expect it to still yield a satisfactory income. Peter and Rachel attempted to cope with change, not by seeking a new occupation but by increasing their geographical mobility and bringing their present occupation to a new locale.

MAKING A LIVING IS DIFFICULT BUSINESS

The inhabitants of San Vicente go about the daily business of making a living as members of households, each collectively focused on one or more livelihood strategies that require the cooperation of all household members to make them work. Fishing and farming are the two main livelihood strategies in San Vicente, but each varies in significant ways. Local residents may fish from the shore or from the ocean, from motorized or from oar-powered boats, or with hook-and-line or with different kinds of nets. Some local residents grow irrigated rice in lowland fields, whereas others grow root crops and tree crops in upland fields. Differences in ethnic background, social class, and gender all help account for these different ways of fishing and farming, which also involve different forms of cooperation within and beyond the household and affect coastal resources in different ways.

Looking back on my fieldwork in San Vicente, the most common theme in my many conversations with local residents was economic hardship. "You cannot sit still and survive," one told me, "you have to be working all the time." But neither is it sufficient just to be hard working. Most fishermen I knew worked long and hard hours, but the rising price of gasoline and declining fish stocks has made fishing an increasingly unprofitable economic activity. Farming was working for some but not for others. And many coastal residents lack farm land, agricultural opportunities, or the appropriate cultural inclinations and skills.

Fishermen and farmers alike agreed that you need to have "more than one thing going for you"—a sideline—but sidelines are difficult to come by. "The world is changing, and you need to change too" is another oft-heard bit of local wisdom. A truism, perhaps, but efforts to cope with change, as I have demonstrated in this chapter, are not easy and they carry the risk of failure. All the efforts of individuals to get ahead, whether by fishing or farming, or by developing a supplementary income activity or even by completely converting to a new livelihood, unfold in households where men and women may experience conflicting ideas regarding how best to proceed. These are some of the principal challenges that San Vicente's residents must overcome as they attempt to survive, and hopefully to prosper, in the early twenty-first century.

ENDNOTE

1. For detailed descriptions of beach seining in the Philippines, see Cañete (2000) and Yano (1994).

5

✳

Enter the Coastal Resource Management Project

In a country that sometimes appears to outsiders to be the land of acronyms, the acronym CRM, for coastal resource management, is one of the most widely heard. Coastal resource management programs in the Philippines characteristically aim to reduce fishing effort to sustainable levels, to halt illegal or destructive fishing practices, and to protect coastal habitats. The emphasis and components of specific CRM projects vary, but the basic idea behind all is to plan, implement, and monitor the sustainable use of coastal resources.

One such project was the Coastal Resource Management Project–Philippines, or CRMP, a seven-year (1996–2002) project that provided technical assistance and training in coastal resource management to local governments and communities. It was funded by the U.S. Agency for International Development (USAID) and implemented by the Department of Environment and Natural Resources (DENR) in the Philippines, in partnership with other national and local government units, nongovernmental organizations (NGOs), and local people's organizations. Though I knew of the USAID connection from the start, only after I began writing this book did I realize that because USAID is federally funded, my own tax dollars were helping to pay for the plan. I have to confess that this realization increased my interest!

The CRMP included a wide variety of activities, some of which I will consider in detail in this chapter. The project's ultimate and decidedly ambitious goal was to catalyze coastal resource management throughout the Philippines by working with a broad section of coastal stakeholders and, in particular, with municipal governments at six different "learning sites" around the country to develop their capabilities to better manage coastal resources. I came to see the project as an experiment in institution building that attempted to fold a new activity (coastal resource management) into an existing institutional structure (municipal government). Palawan Island is shaped and divided into administrative units in such a way that all of its thirteen municipalities have significant stretches of coastline. When I began my research on coastal resource management issues in Palawan in 2002, the CRMP was just ending after a 1-year extension. One of the reasons I selected San Vicente for study from among Palawan's other municipalities was that it had served as one of the project's learning sites. As I have showed in previous chapters, coastal resources in San Vicente are substantially degraded, and local residents who rely on those resources find it more difficult to earn their livings than in the past. The CRMP aimed to do something about these problems, and here I thought was a good opportunity to see what a project might actually accomplish.[1]

THE PHILIPPINE EXPERIENCE WITH COASTAL RESOURCE MANAGEMENT

The CRMP was one of many projects implemented in the Philippines and elsewhere in Southeast Asia following a growing realization that fisheries resource over-exploitation and coastal environmental degradation have complex social, economic, and political origins, and that effectively addressing coastal resource management issues requires fishers and other resource stakeholders to be more involved in the management process. Put differently, widespread agreement now exists that whatever the laws and regulations might be, fisheries management cannot succeed without the cooperation of the men and women who fish to make those laws and regulations work.

The Philippines has a long history of government regulation of the nation's fisheries, and whatever folk notions of resource management or property rights might have existed in the nation's coastal areas have long since weakened or disappeared in the face of technological change and outside political and economic forces. This lack of folk norms is even more evident in Palawan where many fishing communities are of recent origin and composed of migrants of diverse ethnic backgrounds whose ability to establish and enforce norms of fishing behavior through collaborative processes of decision making and rule making are weakly developed. To secure the cooperation of local fishing people in these circumstances requires considerable thought and effort.

The national government's responsibilities for fisheries management were most recently delineated in the National Fisheries Code of 1998 (Republic Act No. 8550), and municipal government authority over local fishing grounds dates back to the colonial period. But ineffectual regulatory measures and lack of enforcement, destructive fishing practices, illegal commercial fishing in municipal waters, and population pressure have all brought Philippine coastal ecosystems to their current diminished state. Since the passage of the Local Government Code of 1991, which devolved greater control over coastal resource access to local levels through policy and institutional reforms, a wide variety of government and NGO-sponsored "co-management" initiatives have attempted to partner various levels of government with local fishing communities in more active and participatory forms of coastal resource management.

Because of the very success of some of these reforms and initiatives, the formal institutional landscape governing coastal resource management programs is muddled. One problem is that national, provincial, and municipal government policies governing coastal resource use sometimes come into conflict. For example, several municipal governments in Palawan attempted to ban the environmentally damaging live fish trade after the provincial government lifted its own ban in 2002. Some proponents of the trade believe that the provincial government has jurisdictional authority in this matter and that conflicting municipal ordinances can be ignored. A wealthy and politically influential businessman involved in the trade is currently challenging one municipal ordinance in the courts.

Another problem is that the boundaries of various NGO programs and donor-assisted government coastal resource management initiatives sometimes overlap. Two environmentalist organizations based in Puerto Princesa City each secured international funding for projects involving the residents of the same twelve fishing communities that line nearby Honda Bay. For a while, both organizations worked simultaneously in all twelve communities, much to the confusion of local residents, but they eventually agreed to split the communities in half for purposes of their respective projects. In San Vicente, the northernmost community of Binga fell within both the USAID-funded CRMP and the Malampaya Sound Land and Seascape Protected Area, one of a series of environmentally critical areas proclaimed under the National Integrated Protected Area System (NIPAS), which was funded by the European Union. CRMP and NIPAS officials clashed politically and personally about which agency was responsible for "protecting" Binga, and in the end, little was accomplished there by either one.

This muddled institutional landscape has also created significant openings for environmentalist action. The Philippines has been a leader worldwide in coastal resource management efforts, and together with the Bahamas, it was the first to implement such programs at the local level. The basic approach appears sound enough. Higher levels of government, sometimes assisted by NGOs, aim to provide the regulatory and infrastructural capabilities that local fishing communities lack, and the fishing residents of these communities in turn must contribute their local knowledge to management initiatives and mobilize their peers in support of those initiatives. Putting this now well-established project design into practice in the Philippines has proven a challenging task and, as I will discuss later, most coastal resource management projects in the Philippines have not achieved their goals.

THE CRMP: OBJECTIVES AND COMPONENTS

As an anthropologist long accustomed to fieldwork in particular locales, whether in hunting-gathering bands, farming communities, or now fishing villages, I contemplated fieldwork on a project that was internationally funded and staffed and was implemented in many locales at the level of an entire country. I was accustomed to participant observation and to speaking directly with the people whose lives I wanted to study. But here was a project that was clearly of great importance to the lives of the people I wanted to study, and yet many of its elements and dimensions lay well beyond the boundaries of San Vicente. Many people involved with its design and implementation I would never meet. The entire Philippine state was clearly an important actor. I could not limit the scope of my fieldwork to San Vicente alone, but where else should I go in such circumstances, and with whom should I talk?

Some anthropologists are today turning to what has been termed "multisited ethnography" to help meet the challenges to ethnographic fieldwork posed by global forces and global interconnections. I knew that the CRMP existed at a variety of different sites and that I would need to investigate at least some of them to fully understand what was happening in San Vicente. For this reason, I eventually visited the project headquarters in Cebu, another learning site, on Negros Island in the Visayan Islands, and the DENR office in Puerto Princesa City. I also exchanged e-mail messages with various government officials and project personnel, listened to a weekly, project-sponsored radio program in Puerto Princesa City, and visited the project website.

From my visits to these sites, I learned about the project design and what it was expected to accomplish nationally. I also learned about the local implementation of various project components, such as the environmental education programs and MPAs discussed later, and the rationale for including each of those components in the project. Here, briefly, is how the project worked. Nationally, the CRMP developed numerous collaborations with various government agencies as it attempted to assist the Philippine government in finding practical solutions to four key coastal resource management problems: jurisdictional issues, mangrove management, commercial fisheries management, and biodiversity conservation. Locally, the goal of the project was to help communities and municipal governments institutionalize coastal resource management planning and implementation as one of their regular governmental responsibilities. In this regard, the project needed to conduct an educational campaign among municipal governments. The Local Government Code of 1991 turned over a considerable amount of authority to local municipal governments for managing their own projects, but many municipalities continue to see coastal resource management as an optional activity or as "someone else's responsibility."

The CRMP's basic goal of catalyzing coastal resource management nationwide was embodied in an ambitious set of project objectives (Figure 5.1). To achieve these objectives in San Vicente, the project joined forces with the municipal government, on the one hand assimilating some of the municipality's own prior initiatives and, on the other hand, attempting to prepare the municipality (in particular, the Municipal Planning and Development Office, or MPDO) to continue to implement the CRMP's larger and more ambitious vision of coastal resource management following the project's termination. The project headquarters for the San Vicente learning site was located in an office building in Puerto Princesa City. Staff members housed in this building had to travel 5 hours by jeep or van to San Vicente. Technical support personnel from one or more of the project's cooperating agencies sometimes accompanied them.

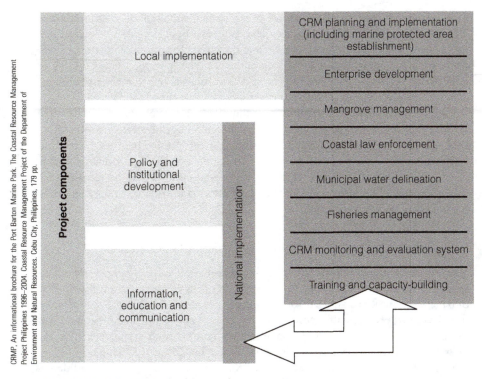

CRMP, An informational brochure for the Port Barton Marine Park. The Coastal Resource Management Project Philippines 1996-2004. Coastal Resource Management Project of the Department of Environment and Natural Resources. Cebu City, Philippines, 179 pp.

FIGURE 5.1 CRMP objectives and components

Coastal Resource Management Planning with the Municipal Government

Central to the CRMP's implementation strategy was a close working relationship with the municipal government. The project recognized that local community participation was an important element of sustainable coastal resource management, and project staff members worked directly with local communities, but the project viewed municipal governments as the legally mandated units to implement coastal resource management initiatives. After the project cycle was complete, municipal governments would be responsible for carrying forth with the coastal resource management agenda. Strengthening the municipal government's capacity to manage coastal resources was the project's major objective. At a series of meetings in San Vicente with the mayor and staff members in the MPDO, project officials proposed and developed a five-phase planning and implementation process, beginning with the identification of issues and a baseline assessment that would require the direct participation of local community resource users.

Based on the results of this assessment, in the second phase of the process, the municipal government prepared and adopted a detailed coastal resource management plan. The plan begins with a detailed profile of San Vicente's coastal environment, drawing on data provided by the CRMP and the Palawan Council for Sustainable

Development (PCSD) about the variety of and present condition of coastal resources. The plan then identifies four "management issues and opportunities": coastal habitat degradation, sustainable fisheries management, sustainable tourism, and lack of alternative sources of income. The last section of the plan, the "plan for action," consists of strategies and activities intended to protect coastal habitats, to promote environmentally conscious enterprises, and to manage fisheries for sustained production.

In the third phase of the planning and implementation process, the municipal government implemented specific programs containing the strategies and activities laid out in the coastal resource management plan. These strategies and activities mostly involved enforcement of existing coastal regulations or enactment of new ones. Outcomes were monitored and evaluated in the fourth phase of the process. The fifth phase consisted of information management, environmental education, and outreach.

Project Initiation and Local Community Acceptance

The CRMP assigned a community fieldworker, herself a San Vicente resident, to spend the first year of the project assessing local needs and levels of understanding of basic environmental issues through informal interviews with local residents. At the same time, project staff members held a series of get-acquainted meetings with representatives of various local "stakeholder" groups, such as the beach resort operators and fishermen's associations discussed in Chapter 2. The purpose of these meetings was to explain the goals of the project and to gain the confidence and cooperation of local residents. The meetings were also an occasion to gauge differences between local stakeholders in their understandings of coastal resource issues and their views of what needed to be done. These meetings took place before I began my research, but I learned that tensions emerged on some occasions because of preexisting conflicts over resources between different user groups and the belief that local stakeholder representatives were themselves involved in the kinds of fishing practices that the CRMP sought to curtail.

Documenting Local Knowledge

To further build community acceptance, a second major project initiative sought to document local knowledge of coastal resources and local understandings of the problems encountered by resource users. With the assistance of local community members, project staff members conducted an extensive participatory coastal resource assessment exercise. As a first step toward the management and protection of coastal resources, participatory coastal resource assessment seeks to identify and value the views and knowledge of coastal resource users regarding coastal habitats, resources, uses, and issues. Although the term *participatory resource assessment* may be unfamiliar, the process is very much an anthropological one. In San Vicente, it involved researchers sitting down with fishing men and women and other coastal resource users, perhaps in a store, a chapel, or someone's front yard on the beach, to talk informally and in detail about what local people know and think about the coastal environment.

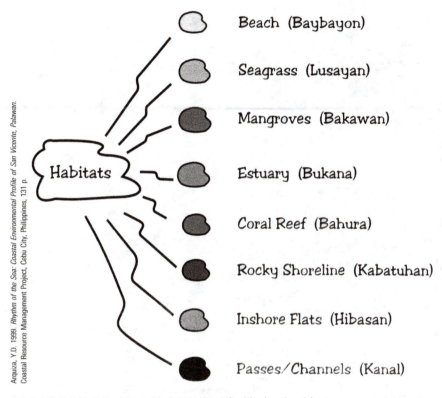

Arquiza, Y.D. 1999. *Rhythm of the Sea: Coastal Environmental Profile of San Vicente, Palawan.* Coastal Resource Management Project, Cebu City, Philippines, 131 p.

FIGURE 5.2   Coastal habitats identified by local residents

The CRMP ultimately produced a handsome volume, *Rhythm of the Sea* (Arquiza 1999), based on the results of this research, and two of the illustrations that appear in this volume are included here. Figure 5.2 shows the different coastal habitats identified by local residents, and labeled with local Tagalog terms shown in parentheses. Several of these habitats—coral reefs, mangroves, and sea grass beds—coincide with the three interdependent ecosystems emphasized by coastal resource managers, as discussed in Chapter 2. Other habitats identified by locals are different. For example, local residents distinguish between sandy and rocky shorelines, and between estuaries and inshore flats, revealing how they often make finer distinctions according to the unique ways in which they make use of their resources.

With the assistance of project staff members, local residents then recorded the local names of all fish and other resources found in each of their named habitats. Most of these fish names appear in Table 4.4 or Appendix A. Local residents and project staff members assigned numbers to these resources and used them in the next step of the participatory resource assessment exercise, preparation of detailed coastal resource maps for each community in San Vicente. Figure 5.3 shows an example of one of these maps for the community of New Agutaya. Four kinds of resource-related information appear on the map: (1) locations of the various coastal habitats (Figure 5.2) found in the community; (2) which of San Vicente's

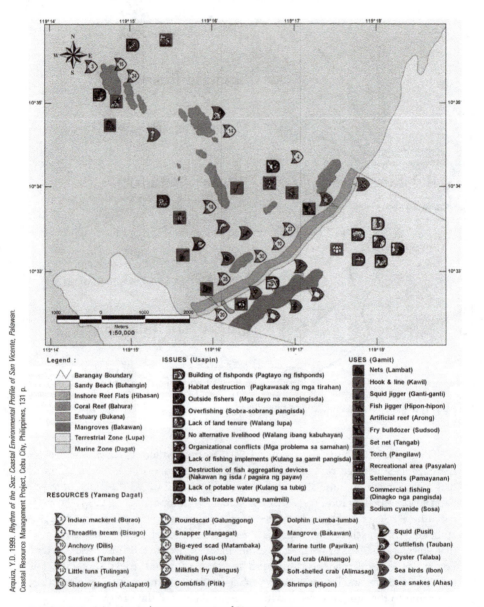

Arquiza, Y.D. 1999. *Rhythm of the Sea: Coastal Environmental Profile of San Vicente, Palawan.* Coastal Resource Management Project, Cebu City, Philippines, 131 p.

FIGURE 5.3 Coastal resource map of New Agutaya

various coastal resources are important locally; (3) the major uses of these habitats and resources by local residents, including some of the fishing techniques I discussed in Chapter 4; and (4) the major issues confronting local resource users. In the case of New Agutaya, these issues range from habitat destruction and the intrusion of outside commercial fishermen to lack of fishing equipment and potable water.

As project staff members worked with local residents in each community on local resource issues, staff members gradually assembled a "master list" of these issues for the entire municipality. They organized the list by relating issues to habitats. For example, oil erosion in the uplands and discharge of domestic waste particularly affected inshore flats and coral reefs, whereas fishpond construction particularly affected mangrove forests. This exercise confirmed that local residents were well aware of how a variety of human activities in or near the coastal zone, in addition to activities in the ocean itself, affected the well-being of fish and other marine animals and plants. Some of the issues raised by local residents went beyond immediate environmental impacts, such as siltation of coral reefs and cutting of mangrove forests, to broader economic, social, and political concerns. These concerns included lack of alternative livelihoods, insecure land tenure, poor nutrition, and lack of health care centers and credit facilities. These concerns show that the understandings of local residents about their resource use problems are both better contextualized and more nuanced than are those of many outside environmentalists, particular in the connections residents draw between resource issues and their everyday lives and livelihoods.

A final task undertaken by the CRMP was to document the decline in local fish catches caused by various negative impacts on coastal resources. I showed in the last chapter how Bruce Lee, Jose, and other fishers all complained that their nightly catches had declined over the years, so much so that they sometimes had little or no fish left to eat or sell after meeting expenses. Policy makers typically require more than anecdotal evidence on which to act and invest money into coastal resource management programs. In the present case, they wanted systematically obtained evidence regarding the extent of the decline in fish catches and the period over which it had occurred. Some local fishing people also needed convincing that environmental problems were serious. This group primarily consisted of those who had only recently arrived from more degraded coastal areas elsewhere in the Philippines and who regarded San Vicente's fish stocks as comparatively abundant. Working with local fishermen in 1997, a CRMP research team prepared a series of "trend maps" that charted, by weight, the fish catches of individual fishermen over time in all ten local communities.

Figure 5.4 shows two trend maps, for Poblacion and Caruray. Fish catches in kilograms per person per day are recorded on the vertical axis, and the years for which information was gathered, 1975 to 1997, are recorded on the horizontal access. Catch figures for years before 1997 are estimates based on the recollections of interviewees. Local fishermen entered notations, some in Tagalog, along the trend lines on each chart, to indicate the points in time at which they believed that population growth, the introduction of illegal or more efficient fishing techniques, and the start of local mining and logging operations on nearby mountainsides began to negatively affect fish stocks. Even allowing for possible exaggeration in the trend lines in Figure 5.4, showing the relative abundance of fish in years past, fishermen in both Poblacion and Caruray evidently experienced dramatic and sustained declines in their average catches, from 30 to 50 kilograms a day in 1980 to about 10 kilograms a day in 1997. These declines are consistent with those reported by my informants in Chapter 4. Comparative information

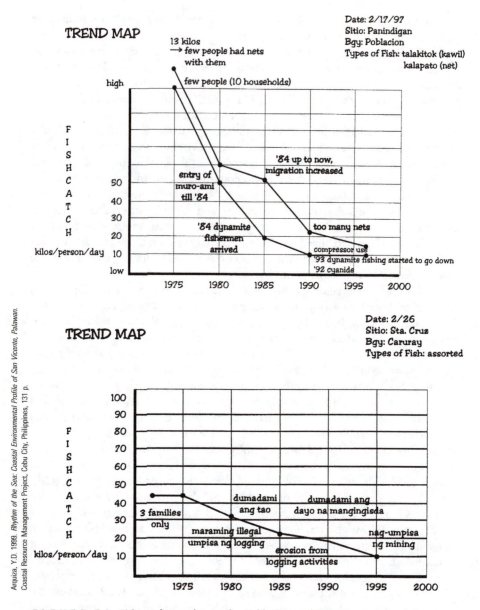

TREND MAP

Date: 2/17/97
Sitio: Panindigan
Bgy: Poblacion
Types of Fish: talakitok (kawil)
                          kalapato (net)

13 kilos
→ few people had nets
   with them

few people (10 households)

'84 up to now,
migration increased

entry of
muro-ami
till '84

'84 dynamite
fishermen
arrived

too many nets

compressor use
'93 dynamite fishing started to go down
'92 cyanide

high

F I S H C A T C H

kilos/person/day

50
40
30
20
10

low

1975   1980   1985   1990   1995   2000

TREND MAP

Date: 2/26
Sitio: Sta. Cruz
Bgy: Caruray
Types of Fish: assorted

F I S H C A T C H

kilos/person/day

100
90
80
70
60
50
40
30
20
10

3 families
only

dumadami
ang tao

dumadami ang
dayo na mangingisda

maraming illegal
umpisa ng logging

erosion from
logging activities

nag-umpisa
ng mining

1975   1980   1985   1990   1995   2000

FIGURE 5.4 Fish catch trend maps for Poblacion and Caruray

from elsewhere in Palawan suggests that in the future the decline could go even further, if excessive and destructive fishing practices are not curtailed. For example, in one of the fishing communities located on heavily fished and degraded Honda Bay near Puerto Princesa City, Rebecca Austin reports that the nightly catches of hook-and-line fishermen declined from 13 to 14 kilograms in 1975 to only 2 to 4 kilograms in 1997 (2003: 119–120).

Arquiza, Y.D. 1999. *Rhythm of the Sea: Coastal Environmental Profile of San Vicente, Palawan.* Coastal Resource Management Project, Cebu City, Philippines, 131 p.

Environmental Education

CRMP staff members viewed environmental education as a task for all. Through the participatory resource assessment activities just described, they sought to educate themselves about local environmental knowledge and local understandings of resource-related problems. They also sought to educate local residents about the extent and causes of these problems and about what might be done to solve them. For example, local residents understood that healthy coral reefs produce more fish, but most did not understand the ecosystemic relationships that make the health of coral reef ecosystems dependent upon the health of nearby mangrove and sea grass ecosystems. Similarly, local residents knew that blast fishing and cyanide use damaged the coastal environment, but many needed to learn the extent of that damage before becoming motivated to take action. Local residents were less familiar with the destructive environmental impacts of highly efficient fishing gear such as Baby trawls and modified Danish seines, which were a particular focus of the educational effort. To help educate local residents about environmental issues, the CRMP sponsored a weekly radio program dedicated to coastal resource issues in Puerto Princesa City and produced the *Rhythm of the Sea* volume discussed earlier. Nationally, the project produced and disseminated several publications on the state of the nation's fisheries and attempted to popularize coastal resource management concepts using comics and posters printed in local languages.

Marine Protected Areas

One of the major initiatives of the CRMP was the planning and establishment of a series of marine protected areas or MPAs, each of which would subsequently be managed by a local fishing community. Also known as fish sanctuaries, no-take zones, and marine parks, MPAs are a popular component of coastal resource management projects generally. The basic goal of MPAs is to enhance and sustain fishery resources, either by protecting healthy marine habitats or by promoting the recovery of degraded ones. MPAs have a no-take zone or "sanctuary" banning the harvesting of fish or other marine life, thereby enabling fish stocks and all marine organisms to mature and thus reproduce at a higher rate. Bigger fish produce many more eggs than smaller ones do, and no-take sanctuaries typically host more and bigger breeding stock, thereby increasing the supply of young fish and leading to a buildup of the fish population. Once fish populations inside the sanctuary recover and increase, fish spill out of the sanctuary and boost the catches of local fishermen. Ocean currents also disperse eggs and juvenile fish to populate other habitats (see Figure 5.5).

Sometimes the purpose of marine sanctuaries is to protect mangroves and sea grass beds, but in the Philippines, they are mostly commonly and visibly associated with the protection of coral reefs, and that was their primary purpose under the CRMP. A healthy coral reef can produce 20,000 kilograms of fish per square kilometer per year, whereas a square kilometer of reef in poor condition can only produce 5,000 kilograms of fish. Of the twenty-two reefs in San Vicente included

FIGURE 5.5 An educational poster promoting marine protected areas

in the PCSD's survey of coral reef conditions discussed in Chapter 3, one was judged in excellent condition, three in good condition, twelve in fair condition, and six in poor condition. Overall, the potential benefits of coral reef rehabilitation there are considerable. To that end the CRMP worked with the municipal government to encourage each local community to establish at least one MPA in its local waters, with the understanding that once those protected areas had been formalized, each community would be responsible for monitoring the compliance of local fishermen and evaluating the progress of the sanctuary in promoting the recovery of fish stocks. By the time the CRMP phased out, seventeen MPAs had been proposed, ranging in size from less than a hectare to more than 10 hectares, but only six protected areas, in Port Barton, Poblacion, and Caruray, had been officially proclaimed by the municipal government. The others were still in various stages of the approval process, which requires local public hearings and prior approval by local community governments before a proposed protected area can be ratified and proclaimed at the municipal level.

Enterprise and Alternative Livelihood Development

The CRMP recognized the need to address the livelihood concerns of fishermen, to reduce fishing pressure with minimal economic hardship. Ideal new enterprises and livelihoods would focus on easily marketed commodities and activities that cause no harm to the environment and are practical for rural households of fishermen and their families (CRMP 2004). The CRMP tried to establish different enterprises in different areas depending on local resources and opportunities. The project's enterprise development efforts in San Vicente, in partnership with the municipal government, included a bottled coconut vinegar project in New Agutaya, bottled "Spanish sardine" projects in Panindigan and Alimanguan, and promotion of seaweed farming in Poblacion and Port Barton. The coconut vinegar project was subsequently abandoned for economic reasons, but the two sardine projects continue. Both are based in small factories that irregularly employ about a dozen women each, depending on the availability of suitable fresh fish for cooking and bottling.

As unlikely as the idea may sound, seaweed farming today is common throughout island Southeast Asia. Wild stocks of seaweed have long been harvested throughout the world, both as a food source and as an export commodity for the production of agar and carrageenan, gelling agents used to thicken, stabilize or emulsify industrial, pharmaceutical, and food products. Among the many everyday products Americans buy that may contain carrageenan are ice cream, pudding, candy bars, processed meat, toothpaste, shampoo, and shoe polish. Beginning in the 1970s and 1980s, demand for seaweed and seaweed products began to outstrip supply and efforts began to increase production by cultivation. In the Philippines, seaweed exports increased almost twentyfold between 1967 and 1980 and then doubled again by 1985, to a level of 28,000 metric tons (Crawford 2002: 1). The province of Palawan presently ranks second in the nation in total production. Introduced first by the municipal government in the early 1990s and later promoted by the CRMP, seaweed farming in San Vicente centers on the cultivation of *Kappaphycus alvarezii* and related species.

F I G U R E 5.6 A woman inspects newly harvested seaweed

Successful seaweed culture requires relatively calm areas of the ocean, such as bays and inlets, free of pollution where moderate currents of appropriate temperature flow consistently to bring needed nutrients. Actual cultivation is simple enough. In water approximately 6 to 8 meters in depth, a farmer floats a set of long lines anchored to the ocean bottom. Discarded pieces of white Styrofoam support the lines and make them easily visible. The farmer then hangs a series of weighted lines from each floating line at regular intervals. A seaweed buyer provides the young seaweed plants, typically on credit, and the grower attaches them at regular intervals to the hanging lines. Under good growing conditions, the seaweed matures and is ready for harvest in about 45 to 60 days. Following harvest, the farmer first dries the seaweed and then sells it back to the buyer, who handles further marketing (Figure 5.6). Seaweed farming absorbs household labor because women and older children do some of the principal tasks. Its environmental impacts are minimal and may even be beneficial, attracting turtles and increasing production of herbivorous fish and shellfish. Potential negative impacts include changes in patterns of sedimentation and water movement, depletion of nutrients, and alteration of natural habitat before planting (Crawford 2002: 3).

The Port Barton Marine Park

The signature initiative of the CRMP in San Vicente was the Port Barton Marine Park. Established jointly with and today managed by the local community government in Port Barton, the park encompasses the whole of Port Barton

Things to do in Port Barton:

✓ Island hopping, beach walking, swimming in the Port Barton Marine Park
✓ Snorkel and scuba dive in the designated sites
✓ Trek or horseback ride to the Pamuayan waterfalls
✓ Explore the mongrove forest of Darapitan River to see bats, monkeys, crocodiles and snakes
✓ Contribute to the local economy by purchasing local goods and services.

PORT BARTON

SAN VICENTE, PALAWAN

HOME OF THE COMMUNITY - MANAGED PORT BARTON MARINE PARK

Things NOT to do in Port Barton:

Ψ Do not buy any wildlife, dead or alive from vendors.
Ψ Do not collect seashells, corals or other wildlife.
Ψ Do not litter.
Ψ Do not enter the core zones
Ψ Do not drop anchor, use the mooring buoys instead.
Ψ Do not touch or break corals.
Ψ Do not harass wildlife.

Donations for the development and maintenance of the Port Barton Marine Park are welcome. Please contact any barangay official or any member of the Park Management Council or the Coastal Resource Management Technical Working Group, Barangay Port Barton, San Vicente, Palawan.

FIGURE 5.7   An informational brochure for the Port Barton Marine Park

Bay (Figure 2.3) and places under protective status resources that include sea grass beds, three species of mangroves, marine turtles, mangrove snakes, sea turtles, and at least eighty-two species of fish. The park serves as a multiple use area zoned for a variety of human economic activities declared to be environmentally friendly, including pearl and seaweed farming, and scuba diving. Portions of the park are open to fishing, but three coral reefs remain as core zones closed to all forms of human activity. Figure 5.7 shows a brochure intended to explain the park to tourists.

THE CRMP: LOCAL PERSPECTIVES
AND RESPONSES

A lot of money and effort went into the CRMP, but as interesting and important as the various project components appear to be, I found myself wondering how local residents felt about the project and the degree to which it had actually affected their lives. By reviewing project documents and interviewing project staff members, I learned a lot about the project, but I felt that I had learned primarily about things that were supposed to happen or were said to have happened. What I had not learned was what had actually happened. For example, a blackboard at the project office in Puerto Princesa City displayed a large grid prepared with chalk, with rows for each of the ten local communities in San Vicente and columns for various project activities, such as "organizational meeting held," "educational campaign conducted," "marine protected area established," and so on. For each activity in each community, a checkmark indicated completion. Even a casual visitor could see at a glance what the project had accomplished and what remained to be done.

As sympathetic as I was to the CRMP effort, I was skeptical of such information. OK, I thought to myself, someone held an organizational meeting, but who attended and how actively did they participate, and did people feel themselves to be organized in a more meaningful way than they were before? And if someone conducted an educational campaign, well and good, but what did people learn from this campaign and how (if at all) had they changed their resource use practices as a result? Again I thought, a MPA may have been "established," but was it working effectively to restore fish stocks? In short, I felt that I was still not finding out what for me was the most anthropologically interesting and significant aspect of all of this, the human dimension.

In the end, I returned to San Vicente and to where I had started, now talking to local men and women about their understandings of the project and about how it affected their lives. Of course, I was interested in determining how "successful" various project components had been, but as an anthropologist, I did not feel that such success could be rated in the simple yes/no fashion of the chart I had seen on the blackboard in the CRMP office. Instead, I would need to consider the perspectives of different local actors, perspectives that I knew might well differ, depending on their particular backgrounds, experiences, and degree of dependence on coastal resources.

Coastal resource management projects in general ask fishermen to curtail certain fishing practices that have proven economically attractive or necessary but that have been judged environmentally undesirable. In other words, these projects require fishermen to make near-term sacrifices for the longer-term benefit of all. But no such project, given preexisting variability in fishing practices, levels of capitalization, and the role of fishing in household economic life, distributes the burdens of conservation equally among all community members. Hence, my main question was about how different people in San Vicente perceived and experienced the burdens and sacrifices called for by the project.

From my previous research in Palawan, I knew that social class, ethnic background, and gender were among the most important dimensions of a person's status in Philippine society, and in my analysis here, I pay particular attention to how these three variables influenced the perceptions of community members about various project initiatives. In so doing, I emphasize local communities as sites of pluralism rather than of social homogeneity, an understanding that runs counter to prevailing management orthodoxies and to the idealized imagery of local communities. More specifically, my findings illustrate how sometimes contentious social interactions across gender, class, and ethnic lines can negatively affect community-based efforts to implement resource management projects (Christie et al. 2003: 22). Local residents agreed that depletion of fish stocks in municipal waters because of illegal and destructive fishing methods is a matter that needs government action. However, they disagreed regarding what precisely needed to be done, and in ways consistent with the social divisions of lowland Philippine society and variations in the degree and kind of household dependence on coastal resources.

Crackdown on Illegal Fishing Activities

I noted earlier that one focus of the CRMP's environmental education campaign was to remind people that environmentally damaging fishing practices were already prohibited by laws that needed greater obedience and better enforcement if fishing stocks were to recover. For some of these practices, the main issue is not pubic acceptance of the prohibitions but the political will and ability to enforce them.

I showed in Chapter 3 that one of the most difficult and widespread coastal resource management issues in the Philippines is the illegal encroachment on municipal waters of large commercial fishing boats using trawls and other highly efficient gear. This pattern of coastal resource use (or misuse) reflects the wider political economy, also discussed in Chapter 3, as marked by a class-based social division between mostly poor and otherwise "small" local residents and wealthy and politically influential "outsiders" based in or near Manila or other large cities who are used to getting their way with natural resources regardless of the law. Although the National Fisheries Code of 1998 reaffirms the long-standing and widely known 15-kilometer municipal fishing waters boundary in the Philippines, intrusions of commercial trawlers into municipal waters are commonplace and, as I discussed earlier, they sometimes occur with the collusion of municipal mayors who are widely assumed to receive a payoff from wealthy boat owners in return for looking the other way.

When the present mayor of San Vicente took office, one of his first political actions was to vigorously pursue commercial trawlers that entered local waters. His effort in this regard was one of the reasons that the CRMP subsequently selected San Vicente among other coastal municipalities in Palawan to be one of its learning areas. Using municipal funds, the mayor purchased a speedboat and set up a system of telescopes to triangulate on the positions of suspected intruders. Municipal authorities regularly boarded and seized commercial fishing vessels and brought their captains to Puerto Princesa City to be charged in provincial courts. Whether this pattern of aggressive detention and prosecution will continue remains to be seen, and even at present, the mayor's political opponents suspect that his motives are not as virtuous as this brief account may make them to appear. Meanwhile, illegal commercial fishing in neighboring municipalities in Palawan continues unabated, and the mayors of those municipalities are widely reported to condone or even to have business involvements in that fishing.

Poor people in the Philippines often complain that the authorities crack down on "little people" for illegal activities, while allowing the "big people" to get away with that same activity, sometimes in return for a well-placed bribe or a "piece of the action." A municipal mayor who stands up to wealthy outside fishing interests to say that they can no longer have their way with the coastal resources in his isolated municipality strikes a blow for class justice. The mayor's enforcement actions were widely popular in San Vicente, even among his political opponents.

After the CRMP and the San Vicente municipal government concluded successful negotiations to establish a joint resource management program, the mayor made a second dramatic political move when he ordered the confiscation of all air compressor rigs in the municipality. Despite denials from their owners, use of compressors is closely linked to the illegal use of cyanide to capture live fish, as I showed in Chapter 3. Municipal authorities ultimately confiscated nearly forty compressor rigs, almost all of them from Visayan fishers in the community of Santo Niño, long regarded as a center of illegal fishing activities. The mayor compensated the owners of the confiscated compressors and invited them to participate in a two-week alternative livelihood training program with a daily honorarium. Fishermen applauded the move, particularly in the neighboring communities of Alimanguan and New Canipo, whose residents were most aware of the damage to local reefs by cyanide fishers from Santo Niño. The mayor, who now jokingly claimed that San Vicente owned more compressors than any other municipality in the country, created significant political support for other elements of the CRMP and the municipality's own coastal resource management efforts.

Limitations on Use of Active Fishing Gear

The CRMP encountered greater resistance to its efforts to encourage local fishermen to voluntarily curtail their use of active and highly efficient fishing gear, to encourage the municipal government to prohibit the use of this gear, and to enforce that prohibition. Much less local agreement existed about what should or should not be done. I showed in Chapter 4 that successive waves of Visayan migrants to San Vicente, introduced active and efficient fishing gear such as baby trawls, modified Danish seines, and fine-meshed nets. The environmental damage caused by such gear is one element of a wider local discourse among Cuyonon and Agutaynen farmers. They attribute much of the degradation of Palawan's fisheries to the illegal or questionable fishing activities of the migrants, including those who have lived in Palawan for many years. Not surprisingly, all the Cuyonon and Agutaynen farmers with whom I spoke about this matter supported the project's efforts to curtail use of the damaging gear.

Most residents of San Vicente are Visayan, rather than Cuyonon or Agutay-nen, and most of them are engaged wholly or partly in fishing. None of the Visayan fishermen I interviewed employed or admitted that they employed questionable fishing gear. I heard a variety of perspectives. A few fishermen denied that such gear caused significant environmental damage. The majority view was that although these gears might be environmentally damaging, they were necessary for making a living.

When I listened to Visayan fishermen defending the use of active or highly efficient gear by others, or to local officials explaining why they did not try harder to curtail the use of such gear even when national or municipal laws were on their side, I recalled how and why many Americans exceed posted speed limits in driving their cars. Some say that those limits are often unreasonably low and deserve to be ignored. Others acknowledge that excessive speed can be dangerous but feel that they have to drive faster than the posted limit because they are short of time or have to keep up with other drivers. The authorities themselves are complicit in a process whereby the culturally acceptable rate of speed in the United States creeps upward. Where I live, most drivers understand that police with radar guns will not ticket them for speeding unless they exceed the posted speed limit by more than 10 miles per hour. What the "real" speed limit is in such circumstances is open to interpretation. In my view, local officials in San Vicente were acting in a way similar to my local police in their attempt to balance enforcement of the law with the exigencies of daily life. What I heard from local fishermen also reminded me of how many American drivers understand that rapid acceleration is environmentally undesirable because it wastes gasoline, yet they do it anyway. "What real difference is it going to make?" is a comment one might hear either from an American driver or a San Vicente fisherman to justify refusing to change their present behavior. They might also remind the listener that there is still a lot of gasoline, or a lot of fish, left in the world.

Gear issues in San Vicente have gender as well as class and ethnic dimensions, and efforts to curtail the use of some fishing practices disproportionately affect women. In Chapter 1, I recounted how I met beach seiners for the first time, and in Chapter 4, I described how two teams of net haulers operate beach seines. These teams number about ten persons each and are composed largely of women and children. According to coastal resource management experts, beach seining causes degradation of sea grass beds and undesirable physical alteration of near-shore sea bottoms. In addition, because the nets employed are fine-meshed, with mesh sizes as small as 0.5 cm, beach seining is associated with a high incidence and alleged waste of "by-catch." For these reasons, laws in the Philippines restrict the use of beach seines, and municipal ordinances in San Vicente ban their use altogether.

Local residents regularly engage in beach seining only in three San Vicente communities: New Agutaya, San Isidro, and Alimanguan. In these communities, it is an important secondary occupation of many poorer women and children. In New Agutaya, where farming is the primary source of income, beach seining by women and children is the most common secondary source of income. Among the forty households in that community included in my household economic survey, four households own nets used for beach seining (Table 4.1), and four-teen households reported income from beach seining as their second most important source of income. Women and children in other households in this sample periodically participate in beach seining as well.

I found a significant gender dimension to beach seining in a coastal economy where men dominate the capture and marketing of fish. Female beach seiners, working either as net haulers or net owners, earn incomes from fishing relatively free of the direct control or supervision of husbands or other males. Beach seining thus has considerable populist appeal, and the municipality does not currently enforce its ban on this activity. Any attempt by the mayor to enforce the ban could prove costly because his political opponents would likely argue that the mayor should not hurt the "small people" (who, after all, are just trying to survive) in his zeal to save the environment. Most but not all local politicians in the Philippines are men, and in the local politics of San Vicente, allowing beach seining to continue is more about the right of the poor to a livelihood than it is about the rights of women.

Differing local perceptions of beach seining also have an ethnic dimension. Most Visayan fishers I encountered wanted to see the practice eliminated, arguing as environmentalists do that seiners capture juvenile fish that would otherwise grow bigger and move out to sea. In contrast, Cuyonon and Agutaynen farmers who raise hogs profit from beach seining done by female family members (see Chapter 4), though they do not engage in it themselves. They defend beach seining as a traditional and nondestructive practice and believe that environmen-talist arguments against it are misguided. Some joined a vigorous counter-discourse about beach seining. They argued that the shallow ocean waters near the beach are not a "nursery" and that the kinds of small fish captured there do not grow bigger anyway; that the fish caught with beach seines do not ordinarily live near the beach but only approach it during certain climatic conditions (a line of reasoning that explains why beach seiners sometimes capture few fish); and that periodically stirring up the ocean floor near the beach is good for the marine environment. I could find no scientific support for these positions. Based on the PCSD's survey of coastal resources that I discussed in Chapter 3, the condition of sea grass beds in San Vicente mirrors that for Palawan as a whole (Figure 3.2). Of the ten beds in San Vicente included in this survey, six were in poor condition and only one was in excellent condition, suggesting that human affects upon them have been considerable.

Unlike support for widely popular crackdowns in the clearly illegal and much-decried activities of outside commercial fishing boat operators and a small minority of local residents believed to engage in cyanide or blast fishing, a lack of popular enthusiasm existed for efforts to curtail use of beach seines and other active or highly efficient gear. I did not conduct a survey on the matter, nor did I tabulate the answers I received, but I regularly asked fishermen, perhaps fifty in all, how they felt about this aspect of the CRMP's agenda. Most were of the opinion that the project was overreaching its authority by telling people not to do things that, in their view, were not illegal, even if they might be environmentally damaging. Some expressed the view that the municipal government should simply crack down on the (truly) illegal activities and let the ordinary person get on with the business of making a living. "Catch the law-breakers and leave the honest people alone" was one frequent comment. From fishermen, I also often heard comments such as, "If everything is prohibited, how will we eat?" Some non-fishermen were more ambivalent; they acknowledged the environmental damage done by certain fishing practices, but they tempered that acknowledgement with comments such as, "It's a big ocean" and "That's the way they have to make a living."

Establishment of Marine Protected Areas

I noted earlier that the establishment of MPAs in each local community in San Vicente was the centerpiece of the CRMP's agenda. The basic idea is to enhance fishing resources by protecting selected fish populations while they recover and increase, ultimately to the benefit of local fishing households. However, in San Vicente the process whereby particular coral reefs came to be designated for protection and hence placed off-limits to local fishermen caused unhappiness and conflict consistent with community, class, and ethnic differences.

The municipal government called on local communities to designate one or more areas for protection, but left the communities themselves to determine which areas. Once the communities selected sites for protection, CRMP staff members and municipal officials completed the process by undertaking a legal survey and providing marker buoys. Although I was unable to attend any of the community meetings held to discuss potential marine protected area sites in San Vicente, I can make comparative observations of the same selection process elsewhere in coastal Palawan. Writing about local perceptions of marine sanctuary proposals in the Honda Bay region, Austin observes that conventional coastal management understandings suggest that the most suitable candidates for sanctuary status are coral reefs that are still primarily intact, but local fishermen and some local environmentalists prefer sites that are already partially degraded to allow them to regenerate (Austin 2003: 297–298). According to Austin, a local view of marine sanctuaries as primarily about food production rather than about biodiversity conservation is one likely explanation for such a preference; another is ease of surveillance and understandable local concern that communities cannot effectively monitor distant sites against intrusion. Based on my own interviews with local residents who remember attending community meetings in San Vicente where potential MPA locations were discussed, both issues figured prominently and strongly influenced meeting outcomes. Although official municipal designation of MPAs is an ongoing process, sites selected and approved to date are all close-to-shore, degraded coral reefs, rather than more distant and pristine reefs.

These site decisions both reflect and exacerbate a local class difference between fishermen owning motorized pumpboats (able to reach relatively distant fishing grounds) and those owning only smaller, oar-propelled outriggers (relying on the closer-in fishing areas). Seen in this perspective, the site decisions are unsurprising. In most local communities in San Vicente, and in all of those that rely primarily on fishing, most fishermen own motorized pumpboats. Among the households I surveyed in Panindigan, for example, twice as many own motorized boats as own oar-powered ones (Table 4.1). Pumpboat fishermen do not exploit the closest reefs because these reefs have long since been depleted of fish. From their perspective, it makes good sense to site the MPAs on the close-in reefs. The outcome was that fishermen who employed oar-power and relied on these close-in reefs—such as those in twelve of the sample Panindigan households in Table 4.1—now found themselves greatly disadvantaged by the prospect of greater travel times.

Growing public awareness of this outcome left the municipal government and the CRMP again vulnerable to the politically dangerous charge that their conservation efforts were hurting the very people that government should endeavor to assist. An informant told me of a case where a local community resident who had initially supported the establishment of a nearby MPA later reversed his position, explaining, "My (poorer) relatives (i.e., those without motorized pumpboats) got mad at me." No aspect of the CRMP agenda caused more local controversy than did the effort to establish MPAs. Although project personnel and municipal government staff members claimed to have organized meetings in all ten communities to democratically select the areas to be protected, some fishermen told me that they held no such meetings or that the meetings were inconclusive. Others objected to the entire idea of marine sanctuaries on the grounds that the government should not tell people where they may or may not fish.

Some local objections to MPAs resembled those I discussed earlier regarding efforts to discourage use of active fishing gear. Some fishermen felt that additional restrictions on fishing activities were unreasonable and unfair. "It's hard enough to make a living as it is," one man told me. According to another, "The government should arrest the law-breakers and leave the honest people alone (to make their livings as they see fit)." Still other local objections followed ethnic lines. I showed in Chapter 4 that some local Cuyonon and Agutaynen residents who are primarily farmers also fish on a part-time basis with a hook and line. Several Cuyonon farmers who fished from small outriggers in this "on the side" fashion resented the complete closure of the close-in MPAs. In their view, only the nets and activities of Visayan fishermen result in damage to coral reefs, so why not just prohibit net fishing in the proposed MPAs and let hook-and-line fishing continue as before.

Approximately half of the fifty fishermen who let me know their views about MPAs supported the idea in principle but believed that it would not work out in practice. Most worried about community's ability to effectively monitor the sanctuaries against intrusions and misuse by those who would continue to fish there because they have "hard heads" or "don't care." They believed that locating a sanctuary close to shore did not solve the monitoring problem because much fishing occurs at night and local communities lack patrol and apprehension capabilities in the darkness. Such skepticism has proven a crucial detriment to sanctuary success in other locales.

Enterprise Development

CRMP and municipal government programs to create new livelihood opportunities were aimed at poorer local residents and specifically those whose livelihoods suffered negative impacts from various project initiatives. To find out more about potential livelihoods, I interviewed several women about their experiences working in the Spanish sardine factory in Alimanguan, where crews of as many as twelve women workers produce bottles of "Palawan's Best Sardines." They enjoyed the work, but their main concern was that it was irregular. The factory bottles tuna and mackerel as well as sardines, but the local supplies of all three fish vary seasonally and according to the weather. The factory operates when sufficient fish are available and closes down for weeks or even months in slack periods before resuming operations. One woman said she no longer wished to work there. It was too disruptive to her daily routine, not knowing sometimes even until the afternoon before whether she would be called to work the next day. Another woman tolerated the irregular nature of the work but wished that it would be more regular.

The promotion of seaweed cultivation in San Vicente has created more employment than the two sardine factories. Presently about forty households in Panindigan and Port Barton depend at least partly on seaweed farming for their livelihoods. The seaweed farmers I interviewed were enthusiastic about it, and local interest in seaweed cultivation appeared to be growing as the economic success of current cultivators has become more visible. As noted earlier, men, women, and older children can all participate in this activity, an important reason for its popularity. Other advantages of seaweed cultivation include the low capital costs because even a small oar-powered outrigger is adequate for travel back and forth to a household's seaweed beds, and the relatively short maturation time allowing the crop to go quickly to the market.

In 2002, I visited Capsalay Island in Port Barton Bay, where a core group of twenty-four households previously dependent on fishing took up seaweed farming in 1999 with technical assistance and start-up materials provided by the CRMP. At the time of my visit, about half of the households in this initial group of project beneficiaries still farmed seaweed; the others had returned to full-time fishing. Still other households, not in the original group, had recently begun to farm seaweed as well. One seaweed farmer, Tomas, paddled me out in his outrigger to his plot of seaweed about a hundred meters offshore. There he had floated several hundred lines, each with seaweed plants at various stages of maturity. This was the third location he had tried, and the yield here was the best yet. We looked at seedlings he had planted the previous day, after purchasing them from a dealer in Poblacion for U.S. $0.10 per kilogram. He told me that his last sales had been at $0.42 per kilogram. On his last trip to the market, he learned that the local buying price had recently increased to $0.46 per kilogram. Tomas's neighbors recently attended a seaweed farming workshop where they heard that seaweed grown in other parts of the Philippines was ready for harvest after 45 to 60 days. Local residents often find, however, that the technical advice they receive at training workshops needs to be modified to fit local conditions, and Tomas has found that near Capsalay Island it is better to wait almost 75 days before harvesting seaweed.

Tomas was not concerned about possible fluctuations in the buying price for seaweed as much as he was about marketing channels and the difficulty of selling it. Seaweed farming had not yet really "taken hold" in San Vicente, and for this reason, there was no full-time buyer in Poblacion or Port Barton. Because he lived on a small offshore island, Tomas often found out too late that a buyer was present. On several occasions, he had to bring his newly harvested seaweed to Puerto Princesa City for sale. Even though it was dried and could be safely stored, he needed to sell it immediately to get the money. Tomas heard that an arrangement had recently been worked out with a trader in Puerto Princesa City to send a buyer to San Vicente on a regular schedule. In this case, growers could adjust their planting and harvesting times and enjoy greater predictability. He liked this idea.

I was unable to collect precise income data from Tomas or other seaweed farmers on Capsalay Island, but Tomas estimated that during some months, sales of seaweed provided as much as a third of his household's cash income. Recently, he had expanded his operation, reassured by his success at his new location and by his children now being older and able to help. Local people regard Tomas as a successful seaweed farmer, but he still sees himself first and foremost as a fisherman. Seaweed farming on Capsalay Island and elsewhere in Port Barton and Poblacion is primarily a supplemental source of income rather than an alternative livelihood (Crawford 2002: 6).

Not all of the men and women I interviewed in fishing households found the idea of seaweed farming attractive. Some were skeptical whether the economic returns attributed to it would be sustained. "It's just a fad," one man said, "it won't last." One woman added that although some seaweed farmers might appear to be prospering today, the bottom might fall out tomorrow. Then they would all be *balik sa uno,* "back to square one." These concerns are not unfounded. Reports of disease-caused die outs suffered in years past by seaweed farmers elsewhere in Palawan troubled some prospective growers. Seaweed, like any world market commodity, leaves local producers vulnerable to world price fluctuations, local supply gluts, and the monopolistic power of regional buyers. I heard that buyers are slowly reducing their prices offered to San Vicente farmers, not because of a declining world market for seaweed, but because growers encouraged to experiment when prices were high now have become dependent to the point that they must continue to produce seaweed, even if the price should fall.

Others were skeptical about seaweed farming for different reasons, at least regarding their own households. Some felt that they could not meet its labor requirements on a regular basis; others worried that they would not be able to find an area to plant the seaweed that was free of the risk of cyanide or other pollution. In the course of asking Tomas and other seaweed farmers about this risk, I was surprised to learn that some fishermen change their engine oil at sea. Tomas personally never had a problem with oil pollution, but he knew of others who had experienced such problems, including one who had lost an entire crop.

Coastal resource managers argue that because small amounts of cyanide or engine oil are harmful to seaweed, the spread of seaweed farming should help to motivate larger numbers of coastal residents to speak out about environmental misbehavior. However, seaweed farming is still new in San Vicente, and the relatively few households that pursue it are mostly poor and politically voiceless.

Like Tomas, almost all of these households regard seaweed farming to be of lesser importance, supplementary to fishing as a source of income.

THE CRMP: PROJECT RESULTS
AND LESSONS LEARNED

Following a 2-year extension, the CRMP ended nationally in 2004. In San Vicente, it effectively ended in early 2002, with a carefully orchestrated turn-over of resource management plans and responsibilities to the municipal gov-ernment. These responsibilities included a survey and approval of the remaining proposed MPAs and development of a zoning system to govern the locations of the growing numbers of seaweed farms, fish pens, and other marine enterprises in Poblacion and Port Barton Bay. At the time of the turnover, two significant budget issues remained unresolved. The first was whether the mayor would or could create a full-time staff position in the municipal government dedicated to implementation of the coastal resource management plan. The second was where local communities would obtain the funding needed to purchase, fuel, and maintain the patrol boats required to monitor the newly created marine sanctuaries against intrusion by outsiders.

What did the CRMP accomplish? The project's own answer to this question is contained in a lengthy final report (CRMP 2004) summarizing its accomplish-ments at the national level without reporting specific outcomes either in the 6 original learning areas or in the approximately 120 other municipalities with which project personnel ultimately worked in some way on coastal resource management issues. The report claimed that for 300 kilometers of Philippine coastline, the project had substantially met most of its key performance objectives and indicators. These indicators included development and implementation of coastal resource management plans by partner municipal governments; training of more than 900 municipal-level staff in the implementation of sustainable resource management; the development of new enterprise opportunities together with appropriate links to credit sources and markets; and an annual investment by municipal governments of 2 to 4 percent of their operating budgets in support of community-based resource management initiatives. This final report also indi-cated that project staff made efforts in some learning areas, not including San Vicente, to periodically measure and document changes in fish abundance and coral cover inside and adjacent to the newly established MPAs.

My own view of the CRMP's accomplishments is limited to San Vicente, seen in 2006 several years after completion of the project and largely through the eyes of local residents. In its local resource management outcomes, the project could boast of several successes. First, commercial fishing boats were still avoiding San Vicente's municipal waters, as evidenced by the reports of fishermen and by the absence of the boat lights on the horizon that would betray their presence. Second, blast fishing and compressor-aided cyanide fishing were less frequent than before the project began. My evidence for this claim is only anecdotal because no fishermen would admit to an outsider like me that he engaged in such illegal practices, nor would fishermen who do not engage in these practices agree to "name names." However, fishermen and municipal officials I interviewed believed that lingering problems with illegal fishing practices in San Vicente could be blamed primarily on intruders from other locales rather than on local residents.

Finally, the project's enterprise-development efforts paid off with modest successes. The two bottled sardine factories continued to operate as they had since they opened, employing small numbers of local women on an irregular basis. In my view, they were unlikely to grow further. The concept is sound enough—to add value to a local resource before sale—and the product is tasty. Numerous such enterprises throughout the Philippines offer similar advantages, but they all face stiff competition from cheap imported canned fish. Supply, production, and marketing limitations suggest that these particular enterprises will remain a periodic and unreliable source of employment for those who work in them. As I indicated earlier, this circumstance is acceptable to some local women but not to others. To the degree that these factories employ women who work as beach seiners, their operation may reduce fishing activities among women.

The promotion of seaweed farming paid off in a bigger way. Larger numbers of people found employment growing seaweed, and many of them reduced their fishing activities. Yet how many people can take up seaweed farming? Besides the earlier-noted concerns about possible downward trends in market demand and buying prices, seaweed farming has limits to growing it successfully. Only some portions of San Vicente's coastline meet the criteria for seaweed production discussed earlier. Seaweed suffers from too much ocean movement as well as too little, and the Southwest monsoon season in the Philippines from July to December sometimes brings heavy seas to Palawan's west coast. Present and would-be seaweed farmers are still experimenting in various areas to determine where seaweed grows best. According to one fisheries expert in Puerto Princesa City, about 5,000 square kilometers of Palawan waters are presently used for seaweed culture, and an additional 15,000 square kilometers have good potential for this purpose. Thus, seaweed cultivation has room to grow.

Project outcomes also included significant failures. It is doubtful that two of the main elements of the project—creation of the Port Barton Marine Park, and designation of a series of MPAs—will sustain themselves over time. By 2006, I observed that both the park and the MPAs still existed on paper but no longer in practice. Some fishermen I interviewed could not identify any MPA in San Vicente. Others knew that several protected areas had been proposed but claimed they were never "finalized," and still others acknowledged that some MPAs had been officially established but were not being "honored." None of the MPAs approved by the municipal government were subject to regular monitoring or evaluation. In Port Barton Bay, most of the marker buoys that the CRMP had donated to the local community to help demarcate use zones in the marine park were missing and presumed stolen. In short, some key elements of the plan were not working.

Changing the evaluation focus from outcomes to process and system (Ervin 2005: 97–100) helps explain why. At the community level, the project ran up against local differences in class, ethnicity, and gender such that the "burdens of conservation" placed on local residents by project initiatives were not equally shared. Local residents were not happy about this circumstance. Despite the series of community meetings held early in the project, community residents felt that they had no opportunity to meaningfully participate in the process of formulating initiatives. They believed that the project had come down from above, through the apparatus of the municipal government.

As explained earlier, Philippine law charges municipal governments rather than local community governments with coastal resource management responsibilities. However, even at the municipal government level, the CRMP never succeeded in completely institutionalizing these responsibilities. By 2006, the municipal government had no office or even a full-time staff person dedicated to coastal resource management planning and implementation in San Vicente, and no separate budget item for these activities. Neither local residents nor the municipal government feel ownership of the project or responsibility for its success or failure. As a result, even the project's modest successes are in jeopardy. Meanwhile coastal resource management in San Vicente continues to rely on the political persona of the present mayor. He will eventually leave office, and there is no guarantee that his successor will share his enthusiasm for coastal resource management programs.

In 2006, I interviewed a staff member of the PCSD who was familiar with the CRMP's experience in San Vicente and who was a specialist in resource management issues. He acknowledged that neither the Port Barton Marine Park nor the series of MPAs established during the project period were a "reality" today. In his view, the project had never successfully "capacitated" the municipal and local community governments to manage these initiatives on their own. He acknowledged budgetary limitations, but indicated the main problem was lack of technical and legal expertise and, hence, the capacity to carry forward with these important elements of the CRMP's agenda.

LOOKING FORWARD

A major obstacle to efforts to build community consensus and capacity to implement coastal resource management programs is that most local community residents believe that other people, rather than themselves, are responsible for environmental degradation. Local people typically refer to these misbehaving "other people" by the generic term *dayo,* which means outsider or foreigner. Locals apply the term broadly to include commercial fishing boat operators intruding on municipal waters, poor fishermen residing elsewhere who periodically fish in local waters, and even (depending on the context) resident fishermen who originated in other parts of the Philippines. Based on evidence I collected, I have little doubt that many outsiders behave in environmentally damaging ways. At a discursive level, however, this frequently uttered proposition may be deployed to obscure another truth and absolve local residents of responsibility for environmental damage. If outsiders are the cause of the damage, then they are the ones who should be monitored and reminded of the environmental rules. Local people tend not see themselves as the ones who need monitoring.

Another discursive obfuscation that helps insulate local residents from culpability in environmental degradation is the often-heard proposition that people need to make their livings. Although some people may cause environmental damage, they have no choice if they and their families are to survive. As I have indicated earlier in this chapter, some local residents may acknowledge that their collective actions cause environmental damage and agree that something should be done about it, but they still fail to agree regarding what should be done, expressing their views consistent with class, ethnic, and gender differences in the rural Philippines. And local officials and project managers, finally, may engage in discursive obfuscation as well, when they blame project failures on technical problems or insufficient funds without addressing the more fundamental social and cultural factors that lie at the root of project success or failure.

The CRMP entered this ambiguous and conflicted terrain unprepared for the difficult and time-consuming groundwork needed to build local consensus about what should be done and to ensure that in the end, local leaders would be ready to assume ownership of the project and keep it running and working. Instead, like other large, bureaucratic and "top-down" organizations, the project focused on activities rather than results, or at the least it appeared to confuse the two, such that project staff members regarded the delineation and municipal proclamation of a MPA as a project "accomplishment," regardless whether the protected area worked as intended or not. For this and other reasons discussed in this chapter, the accomplishments of the large and ambitious project in San Vicente were limited. Five years after the project ended, local residents remained without sustainable management of their diminishing coastal resources.

ENDNOTE

1. Further information about the CRMP may be found at www.oneocean.org, the official website of the Department of Environment and Natural Resources for coastal resource management in the Philippines. The website has a link to the CRMP archives, where web pages present useful information about coastal habitats, marine biodiversity, and other coastal resource management-related matters. The website was constructed with USAID support.

6

✳

New Ways of Living

One morning I was walking past a small house near the beach in San Vicente and heard a commotion inside. Curious, I soon discovered a small but enthusiastic audience of family and neighbors crowded around a television set to watch a basketball game. Basketball is wildly popular in the Philippines, but this was not an ordinary game. It was a live telecast of game five of the 2006 NBA finals between the Dallas Mavericks and the Miami Heat, received on a small satellite dish. After I expressed some interest of my own, the owner of the house invited me to stay and watch, and much to my pleasure, both for the chance to make some new friends and because it proved such a good game. After I identified myself as a Phoenix Suns fan, a team that had been eliminated by Dallas in an earlier playoff round, I found myself in conversation with several local fishermen who knew as much or more than I did about the Suns players. One who seemed particularly friendly I looked up several days later about my research.

Much has been written about the impact of global communication technologies and the information they bring on the lives of local peoples. This was not a topic I had set out to study but was instead an aspect of San Vicente life that I just happened upon now and again, as in the case of my chance encounter with the NBA game. Only a small minority of better-off local residents actually own satellite dishes and subscribe to cable television. On the other hand, many residents of even modest means own televisions, and many of these are hooked up to informal cable networks of five or ten households that some satellite television subscribers have set up for a small monthly fee, to help defray their own subscription costs. And in a country where cell phones are truly ubiquitous and whose citizens send more text messages than any others in the world, cell phones are a common sight in San Vicente (see Figure 6.1).

This chapter continues my exploration of the different ways that men and women in San Vicente experience global forces. The Coastal Resource Management Project (CRMP), of course, was an example. Funded in Washington, D.C., implemented from Manila, and directed from Cebu City, the CRMP was motivated by international concern about marine biodiversity conservation and reached down to local communities in San Vicente to influence where and in

Courtesy of James F. Eder

F I G U R E   6.1   A store in Port Barton with a satellite
TV dish

what manner individual fishermen could fish. Many global forces, however, unfold independently of state sponsorship or influence, and seen in the context of everyday San Vicente life, this project was just one of many globally driven processes of change that local residents today engage. Further, some of these global change processes have significant social and cultural dimensions that merit attention because they in turn affect how people use resources, earn livelihoods, and organize their lives. In short, globalization has brought new ways of making a living, such as seaweed farming, to San Vicente, and it has brought new notions about what kind of life to live.

As I consider these new ways of living here, I shall continue to emphasize the important and, often, the lead role of women in setting households in new economic and social directions, especially in circumstances of economic adversity. Alma, the woman I introduced in Chapter 4 who had insisted, despite her husband's skepticism, on bringing a load of dried fish to Manila hoping to realize a greater profit on its sale than she would locally, spoke frankly with me about her motive. "A (married) woman is supposed to be in charge of a household's money, but what if there is no money? Others might just sit there but not me."

MICROFINANCE PROGRAMS

Alma had sufficient money that she was able to finance her Manila venture entirely from household resources. The same was true of Edna and her silkworm project, which I also discussed in Chapter 4. For other rural women having "no money" is not just an expression. Even when promising new livelihood ideas may be at hand, poverty and lack of money to use for anything other than day-to-day living expenses severely constrain the ability of many local residents to experiment as Alma or Edna did with new ways of making a living. Southeast Asia's coastal dwellers typically produce much of their own food, and they are not as "poor" as their limited cash incomes might imply. Local costs of living are also different. However, most of them need any cash they have on hand for food and other daily consumption needs or for small emergencies and other unanticipated expenses, not for investment in new economic activities.

A measure of how scarce cash is in the rural Philippines is that even small amounts of it can be meaningful for investment purposes. In the United States, I would be hard pressed to imagine any viable business enterprise that I could start with only $200. In the rural Philippines, however, 10,000 pesos (the approximate equivalent of $200 in the local currency) could be used to capitalize a variety of household-based income-generating activities. But where would a household in San Vicente get such money? For many residents, better-off relatives may be a source of short-term loans in the event of an emergency, such as an illness requiring a visit to the hospital, but to capitalize a new economic venture, local residents who lack sufficient savings of their own would have to turn to the informal credit market and to local moneylenders. Loans from these sources are costly. In one typical arrangement, locally known as "5/6," a borrower must return 6 pesos for every 5 pesos borrowed after an agreed-upon period, usually 2 weeks. Loans under such conditions are a last resort for local residents, and none would take out such a loan to capitalize a business enterprise because few such enterprises could return money fast enough to meet the burdensome interest rate.

Microfinance programs are new ways of financing economic enterprises, made possible by the spread of various government and private small enterprise loan programs. Inspired by and modeled on the example of the Grameen Bank of Bangladesh and currently very popular in global development circles, microfinance programs aim to provide the poor, and particularly women, with access to credit to stimulate household-level entrepreneurial activity. Microfinance programs have proved to be so significant to the well-being of poor people worldwide that the United Nations declared 2005 to be the "International Year of Microcredit," and in 2006, the Grameen Bank and the bank's founder, Muhammad Yunus, shared the Nobel Peace Prize. According to Lynne Milgram,

> Microfinance programs extend financial services for self-employed
> livelihood projects to those who are not bankable by tradition criteria
> of collateral and income; and access to loans is dependent upon
> participants' membership in self-regulating borrower groups. Programs
> typically target women for household-level enterprises because of

women's well-established propensity to pay back their loans and to contribute their earnings to household well-being. (2001: 212)

I have included such programs in a chapter on "new ways of living" partly because the idea of borrowing money for investment rather than consumption purposes is new for many San Vicente residents and partly because there is a novel social dimension to how microfinance programs operate—the self-regulating borrower groups, in the previous passage—that many local women find attractive.

Two microfinance organizations currently operate in San Vicente. One, *Taytay sa Kauswagan, Inc.* (TSKI) is private and functions in the manner of a widespread traditional form of social organization known to anthropologists as a "rotating credit" association, whereby association members each contribute small amounts of cash to establish a common fund and then take turns borrowing from it. The turns are determined by drawing lots. The Cooperative Bank of Puerto Princesa City sponsors the second microfinance organization and does not require prospective borrowers to pay into an account first. Otherwise, the two organizations function in a similar fashion. Prospective borrowers form local groups that meet regularly to discuss proposed projects and jointly approve the specific loan requests of individual members.

What ideas for microenterprises do San Vicente women propose about how to put these small loans to work? Many women want to open small stores or local buy-and-sell operations, and they seek loans to capitalize their initial inventories, sometimes with products that global influences have made more attractive locally. In Alimanguan, one loan of this kind was to Tony's wife Winnie, who purchased a small inventory of Avon cosmetics to resell to her friends and neighbors. Another was to a woman in New Agutaya who hoped to become a cell phone dealer. Other people seek loans to develop better ways of marketing products. A woman in Alimanguan bought a motorbike for her husband to transport fresh fish from San Vicente for sale in Roxas, about 30 kilometers away, where it would command a higher price. Another woman hoped to become a regular supplier of baskets woven from local materials to a tourist-oriented "native crafts" store in Puerto Princesa City, and she obtained a loan to cover her transportation and shipping costs. Still other women used their loans to buy additional fishing equipment for their husbands or (in the case of one woman whose husband had died) to hire labor to prepare a rice field and harvest cashew nuts.

First-time borrowers are eligible for loans of $60. Each time after repaying a loan on schedule, typically 3 months, a borrower qualifies for twice the amount the next time. Loan repayments are tightly scheduled a week or two apart, and if a borrower misses a payment, the group must make it on her behalf. Microfinance programs are popular in San Vicente. In Alimanguan alone, with about 500 households, more than sixty men and women were participating in the TSKI program and another fifty were participating in the Cooperative Bank program. According to an official at the Cooperative Bank in 2006, there were 123 bank borrowers in San Vicente, mostly in the communities of Panindigan, New Agutaya, and Alimanguan.

Such programs are not without controversy. The most common complaint I heard in San Vicente was that repayment schedules were too short and too strict to make effective use of the loan. According to one aspiring storeowner, "You barely have time to buy your inventory, much less to sell any of it, before the first payment is due." Winnie told me that she only proposed to become an Avon representative after realizing that her initial plan, to buy a piglet and fatten it for sale, was not practical because she would have to pay back the loan before the pig was ready for market. She doubted that she would apply for a new loan once she had paid off her current one. Some residents also observed that the loans were structured in a way that made it difficult to determine the true interest rate, and they suspected that the actual cost of the loans was greater than it appeared. According to an official at the Cooperative Bank, interest rates on their loans are about 2 percent monthly. Other informants objected to the TSKI program requirement that participants first contribute their own money to establish a common fund, before obtaining a loan. One told me that she thought the whole thing was a "racket." "What kind of loan program is that," she said, "where you have to loan them the money? They're the ones who are supposed to loan us money!"

What impact do the microenterprises supported by these loans have on resource use and the environment? Certainly some of them successfully provide many households with a supplementary source of income, and Chapter 4 emphasized the importance to household well-being of such secondary income sources as Winnie's Avon products business. However, the microfinanced enterprises that I encountered in San Vicente were too small to constitute alternative sources of livelihood that would induce a fisherman to stop or even reduce his fishing effort. Some, like the basket-making enterprise discussed earlier, which drew on local stocks of bamboo and rattan, could conceivably even increase pressure on resources if they ever grew significantly in scale.

Most microenterprises in San Vicente funded by these two microfinance programs appeared environmentally neutral, but some promised to reduce pressures on fishing stocks. Sylvia, the wife of a fisherman in Panindigan, borrowed money from TSKI to buy pots, pans, and plates and open a small canteen. She had observed that because of its importance as a local center for marketing fresh and dried fish for residents of other fishing communities, Panindigan attracted many visitors during the day. Most arrived and left by pumpboats. Those who lacked relatives there had nowhere to eat lunch except at several dining stalls in the small public market in Poblacion, about a kilometer away. Sylvia saw a business opportunity here. At least some of the growing number of people who visited Panindigan each day needed to buy lunch, and they would save the additional gasoline expense of traveling to Poblacion by eating at her canteen.

When I last visited Panindigan, Sylvia's Canteen—that was its name—was thriving. There were still slow days, but recently business had been so good that she had hired a second kitchen worker. Her main concern was the high cost of the fresh pork and beef she needed to buy each day to prepare the food she offered her customers. She had to travel herself each day to buy these ingredients at a small market in Poblacion. Sylvia's latest plan was to convince her fisherman husband, who had spent his entire adult life as a fisherman, to stop fishing and to instead raise pigs, so that she would have her own close-at-hand source of pork for her canteen. "He's still thinking about it," she laughed, when I asked what she thought would happen, but if it did happen, this is an example of the kind of small enterprise that would reduce pressure on marine resources.

Sylvia's canteen is likely still thriving, but not all microenterprises are so successful. The failure of microfinance programs, despite their promise to propel large numbers of women out of poverty has attracted considerable scholarly attention (see, e.g., Brett 2006 and Milgram 2001). John Brett (2006) found that many of the small enterprises women started with loans from the small microfinance organization he studied in Bolivia failed to generate sufficient income even to repay their loans, and women instead had to draw on household resources for that purpose. Despite the economically burdensome nature of this particular microfinance program, it remained popular with women. Among the reasons he identified for the continuing popularity of the program was its earlier-noted "social dimension":

> Women valued highly the opportunity to gather with other women, independent of men. This was a time of problem solving, commiseration, camaraderie, mutual support, and pleasure in one another's company. There are few venues of opportunities ... for women to gather outside the context of home or family. Many women very much look forward to the meetings every 15 days and the meetings themselves are a time of animated discussion, laughter, quiet discussions in small groups, and more laughter. (2006: 17)

Stephan Smith (2005) similarly believes that the direct economic benefits of microfinance program participation may often not even be the most valuable result to women themselves. "When participation in microfinance programs leads to improvements in the lives of poor women, the key reasons may be the value of group solidarity, and even the raised self-esteem simply from success in repaying the loans, rather than the microcredit itself" (2005: 21).

As an American and perhaps also as a male, I have trouble imagining how I would ever want to participate in a group of borrowers, much less one required to meet regularly to openly discuss my investment plans and those of others in the group. I regard my credit and loan history as a very private matter. However, several women in San Vicente told me that the "social side" of the TSKI and Cooperative Bank microfinance programs had motivated them to participate. I never attended any of the meetings of borrowers that these two groups sponsored, but my interviews with individual program participants are consistent with the observations of Brett (2006) and Smith (2005), regarding why such programs appeal to rural women in particular, and apply as well in San Vicente.

OVERSEAS EMPLOYMENT

Another important source of funds to finance local economic enterprises in the rural Philippines is remittances from Filipinos working in other countries. Today, more than one million overseas Filipino workers, or OFWs, are working abroad temporarily, and the Philippines has surpassed Mexico as the largest source of migrant labor in the world. In addition, millions of other Filipinos live and work abroad permanently. In 2006, Filipinos working temporarily and permanently abroad contributed in excess of $12 billion to the Philippine economy, more than 10 percent of that nation's gross national product (GNP). About one-fourth of overseas workers are sailors, and the remainder are working in such nations as Saudi Arabia, the United Arab Emirates, Italy, Japan, Hong Kong, Singapore, and Taiwan in occupations that include nursing, cooking, housekeeping, and construction and engineering.

Despite the considerable importance of remittances by overseas workers to the Philippine economy as a whole, relatively few San Vicente residents have sought or found employment abroad. If overseas employment continues to figure as prominently in the Philippine economy as it does now, this circumstance will likely change, as improvements in communication and transportation link local residents more closely with sources of information and recruiters in Manila and Puerto Princesa City. For now, San Vicente is too remote for most local residents to consider overseas employment a practical alternative to their present occupations.

Nonetheless, some local residents have found jobs overseas. In 2005, about a hundred local Visayan fishermen left to work in the Taiwanese fishing industry, but working conditions proved difficult, supervision strict, and the pay not what was promised. Most returned home before completing their contracts. I interviewed several overseas workers who had worked in other countries. I was aware of several others who were abroad at the time of my fieldwork or had aspirations of leaving.

I met one young woman who had recently returned from Japan, where she had worked as an entertainer (*japayuki*). The lodging house where I sometimes stayed in Poblacion doubled as a karaoke bar, and she stopped by one night to offer a song—Debbie Boone's "You light up my life," a local favorite. She had a pleasing voice, and we chatted briefly afterward about her experiences in Japan. Compared with others, her case seemed rather sad. At one time, she had a boyfriend and plans to marry, but after she was recruited for the position in Japan, he abruptly married someone else. Uncertain whether she could return to Japan because of visa problems, and limited by her age (33 years), her job prospects in Japan were few. In Poblacion, she was living off her savings and did not seem to have much in the way of local employment possibilities either. Fairly or not, many Filipinos believe that Filipinas who work in Japan as entertainers enter into sexual relationships with Japanese men to augment their income. For this reason, and because she had taken up drinking and smoking cigarettes in Japan and dressed in a way that was considered immodest by local standards, she had no local marriage prospects. Neither could she easily move to a city, such as Puerto Princesa or Manila, where she might better fit in, because her other siblings had married and left her to care for their ill mother.

I met a young man who began working as a mechanic in Kuwait after finishing a vocational course in auto mechanics in Manila. His father had paid for his vocational training from the money he earned as a fisherman and part-time truck driver. By the time I visited the family, his father had become a farmer. Using money his son had remitted from Kuwait, the father had recently purchased 3 hectares of prime irrigated rice land. He was still "learning to plow," but he considered his economic circumstances much improved. Yet another overseas worker was the wife of the fish pen caretaker I mentioned in Chapter 3. He had asked me to take the photo that appears in Figure 3.1 so that he could send it to his wife in Singapore where she was working as a maid.

The overseas worker I came to know best was Grace, a young Agutaynen woman. I first met her quite by accident on the day I participated in beach seining in New Agutaya. Grace was standing right behind me in the team of seine pullers, and to my considerable surprise, I learned that she had just arrived from Hong Kong the previous day. About 140,000 Filipinos presently work in Hong Kong, mostly as domestic helpers, and Grace was one of them. She returns home every 6 months for a 10-day vacation, and on this particular day, she had decided to join friends and family members on the beach, not out of economic necessity but out of nostalgia for a local subsistence activity she remembered from years past. Grace was single and an oldest daughter, and most of the money she remitted was to help support her parents and to pay the high school tuition of two of her younger siblings. She had also accumulated savings of her own, and although she would not tell me how much, the amount of joking I heard about it among the other seine pullers implied that she might be doing quite well for herself. Grace liked living in Hong Kong, and her employer treated her well. She thinks about returning and settling permanently in San Vicente someday, but she was noncommittal about her future. "In the end," she laughed, "I'll probably just marry a fisherman, but for now I want to enjoy life."

EVANGELICAL RELIGIOUS CONVERSION

At first glance, the topic of evangelical religious conversion may seem distant from the livelihood and resource use issues that are the subject of this book, and I certainly regarded the topic that way myself when I started my fieldwork in San Vicente. As I got to know people better, however, I began to see significant local connections between religious belief and practice and efforts to cope with global forces, including economic ones. I also began to see more clearly that local social life centered on other communities and groups besides the ten territorially bounded and politically defined communities I had initially set out to study. Like the small local communities of borrowers formed by the microfinance programs, these communities might not have distinct territories or physical boundaries, but they were nonetheless a potential source of influence on people's notions about how to earn a living and about what kind of life to lead.

A significant trend in the Philippines is the growing variety and importance of church congregations, Bible study groups, and other religious communities. Protestant churches in particular have experienced remarkable membership growth throughout the country in recent decades, and this has been the case in

Courtesy of James F. Eder

FIGURE 6.2 An evangelical church in Alimanguan

San Vicente as well. I was not so much surprised that many San Vicente residents no longer identified as Catholics as I was by the sheer variety of churches. It seemed that I could walk down almost any small street in San Vicente and soon pass a small church. Some had names I recognized, such as Baptist or Adventist or Pentecostal, but others had unfamiliar names, such as Jesus Is Lord, Christian Fellowship Tabernacle, Born Again, Good News, and End Times (Figure 6.2).

What accounts for the growing popularity of these and other such churches in San Vicente? Only a single Catholic church served each of San Vicente's ten local communities. I reasoned that the congregations of the diverse small evangelical churches might be disproportionately composed of Visayans and other peoples of more distant migrant origins, people who had experienced relatively greater disruptions in their lives than had Cuyonon and Agutaynen. Migrants might be less likely to stick with the social "status quo" and cultural tradition, including Catholicism.

This hypothesis I could test against data from my two forty-household surveys in Panindigan and New Agutaya (see Chapter 2). In those surveys, I recorded the religious affiliations of the household co-heads separately because husbands and wives do not always attend the same church. Potentially, then, I could have eighty religious affiliations to report for each community, but the totals for each were less because some households are headed by single individuals and some respondents declined to answer. In New Agutaya, where half the residents are Agutaynen and many others come from some other part of Palawan (Table 2.2), forty-nine household co-heads identified as Catholic and twenty-two co-heads identified as members of one of the local Protestant churches. In Panindigan, whose residents come from all over the Philippines, the results were in the expected direction but not that different—thirty-six co-heads identified as Catholic and thirty co-heads as Protestant. Table 2.2 shows that in New Agutaya, a substantial minority of residents are of Visayan origin and trace their origins to Negros Island. I separately compared the religious affiliations of these Visayan migrants with those of their Agutaynen neighbors, but the results, though again in the expected direction, were similarly inconclusive.

Despite the limited support for my idea from these findings, I later visited the parish priest, himself of Visayan origin, curious to know what he might think from the perspective of his own 8 years of experience in San Vicente. I asked if he felt that those who have left the Catholic church for other denominations might be disproportionately of Visayan origin. "An interesting hypothesis," he told me. I further explained how I had arrived at it, but he did not think it was true. However, he went on to point out, "Visayans took the lead" in establishing the non-Catholic churches in San Vicente and that "most" of the early converts to these churches had been Visayans. These comments suggested to me that there might still be merit in my "hypothesis," but that I needed to consider other possible reasons for religious conversion besides ethnic ones.

In my previous research in a rural farming community elsewhere in Palawan, I noted a significant gender dimension to evangelical conversion (Eder 1999). Some married women found evangelical Protestantism particularly appealing because it forbids smoking, drinking, and extramarital sexual relations, activities that many married men in the Philippines engage in but which erode household economic well-being and can cause husband-wife discord. According to this perspective, first advanced by Elizabeth Brusco's research on evangelical conversion and the machismo complex in Latin America, women convert to Protestantism and, with the support of other converts, subsequently lobby their husbands to convert as well, to improve their domestic lives and the economic well-being of their children by redirecting into the household the economic resources that their husbands had previously spent on now-forbidden pastimes (Brusco 1995: 5).

I saw evidence for this interpretation of evangelical Protestantism's appeal in San Vicente as well. I learned of several cases where women had begun to attend Protestant churches in San Vicente ahead of their husbands and then, over time and with the help of other church members, convinced their husbands to attend as well. Nellie, whose family I stayed with in Alimanguan and who today attends the End Times Church together with her husband and children, spoke explicitly and enthusiastically about how conversion had changed her husband and their economic circumstances. She told me that he was once "addicted" to gambling. He attended cockfights at every opportunity and played cards with other fishermen several nights a week. "Of course," she added, "he had all the other vices too," referring to the smoking and drinking that men who gamble typically also engage in. Nellie did not seem to feel that these activities were morally wrong so much as they were "luxuries that we couldn't afford"—that is, her husband was spending money on himself that the family needed for household expenses and for the children. According to Nellie, a breaking point came when her husband gambled away a sum of money needed the following week to make the high school tuition payment of their oldest child, leaving her in despair. A female cousin, the wife of the pastor of the End Times Church, suggested that a change of churches might lead to a change of behavior, and Nellie began to attend church there together with her children. Her husband initially continued to attend a Catholic church, but after several months, he converted as well and, with the support of church members, finally gave up his various "vices." Now, Nellie told me, "Everything we earn stays here at home." For people like Nellie, conversion to evangelical Protestantism promises to help relieve the squeeze on household economic resources by eliminating gender-linked patterns of expenditure that are portrayed as immoral or wasteful.

Not all the converts to evangelical churches appeared as concerned as Nellie with the instrumental benefits of conversion for their families. As I thought about religious conversion further, and spoke with other men and women in San Vicente about their motives and experiences, I saw other forces at work. I was struck by the close social ties connecting the members of specific congregations to each other and the associated feelings that converts expressed to me about how they felt their lives now mattered in a way that they had not experienced before they converted. In these accounts, I noticed less about gender and economic strategizing and more about the importance of family and a meaningful life.

Both members and nonmembers spoke to me of the family-like atmosphere of San Vicente's small Protestant churches, where church leaders emphasize equality and humility and individual churchgoers feel important and wanted in a nonhierarchical setting. Some nonmembers saw this in a negative light. They told me that evangelicals only make people feel important to draw converts from among "the ignorant," "the easily influenced," and "the insecure." Other non-members saw these churches more favorably, citing the enhanced self-esteem that many converts apparently experience. I found myself more persuaded by this latter perspective on evangelical conversion.

Other forces are at work as well. The longer services and more participatory nature of many Protestant services provide positive opportunities for self-expression that are otherwise lacking in the lives of many rural dwellers. These opportunities may be particularly welcome at a time of rapid global change when many ordinary rural dwellers feel that they are being left out or driven to the sidelines by global forces beyond their control. Some scholars have argued that Pentecostal Christianity in particular has been so successful attracting converts worldwide because it is "deterritorialized." Unlike Catholicism, with its place-based centers (e.g., the Vatican) and structure of authority, Pentecostal Christianity is not tied down to any one place. Pentecostalism and other evangelical religions succeed because even in remote locales such as San Vicente, they produce a "global citizenry," composed of members who feel that they are engaging with modernity and the outside world on more equal terms (see Jacka 2005: 644).

One element of outside engagement in San Vicente concerned rights to coastal resources and was embodied in statements I sometimes heard along the lines of "God put fish (and other resources) on earth for people to use." Although such statements may appear in a variety of religious contexts, in San Vicente, I most commonly heard them advanced by members of the small evangelical churches to assert the moral rights of poor people to access natural resources on an equal footing with conservationists, rich people, and others, and to use those resources as they see fit. By no means is moral or political commentary on resource use the main business of these evangelical churches aimed at conversion and salvation, but I do think that the messages of engagement and equality that some members hear in these churches encourage them to frame their views and speak out in this fashion.

GLOBAL CHANGES AND LOCAL LIVES

There are others ways to build social relationships, engage the outside world, and discover meaning in life besides religion, and I would be remiss if I did not emphasize that most local residents, whatever their religious affiliations, continue to find pleasure and to experience meaningful lives in the context of their own families and traditional social and cultural practices. As an anthropologist, I studied traditional practices as well. My own greatest pleasures during my fieldwork arose when families invited me to join in their ordinary, everyday social activities. I especially welcomed such opportunities when they entailed boat rides. Local residents use their pumpboats primarily for fishing, but they also use them for a variety of family errands and outings and, most pleasurably from my own perspective, for trips to the beach. Sometimes, these trips were only for a quick swim at a nearby beach 30 minutes away. On other occasions, I joined daylong excursions to remote and isolated beaches or offshore islands several hours away, usually setting a troll line en route with the hope of catching lunch. Sometimes it rained on us, and more than once I returned home with a bad sunburn, but I found these family trips a welcome respite from fieldwork and altogether marvelously enjoyable occasions.

I have joined such family outings on many occasions from the time I first went to live in the Philippines, and I have long been struck by their seemingly "timeless" nature. On one recent trip I joined, a teenager brought along a cell phone to stay in touch with friends back on shore. At first I was bothered and felt that the cell phone was out of place, but I later concluded that it was unimportant. By far the most significant aspect of these traditional family outings was that they involved family members spending time enjoying themselves together (Figures 6.3 and 6.4).

Family outings, cell phones, beach resorts, seaweed, evangelical churches, beach pebbles, fish pens, silkworms, and overseas maids; what do we make of such disparate images of contemporary San Vicente life? Many scholars would say that this is the nature of globalization and of modern life. Much contemporary writing is about the hybrid cultural forms that have emerged in today's world at

Courtesy of James F. Eder

F I G U R E 6.3 Two friends go for a boat ride

the countless intersections of the global and the local and of the modern and the traditional. Cell phones in outrigger canoes and satellite TV dishes atop palm-thatched huts would be but two examples of such "hybridity" in San Vicente.

These contrasts may catch the attention of outside observers, but they are not the aspects of global change that most concern local residents. Reflecting now on my own conversations with local residents about the impact of global change on their lives, I found one of the most common themes was that globalization is not working so well for *them*. They say global changes are degrading their resources and undermining their livelihoods. Sometimes, their point is that outside people are profiting from local resources, but not local people. "They are the ones progressing, not us," was how one local fisherman expressed this thought to me. Afterward, I thought of the beach pebble business and the outsiders who had come to collect pebbles locally. Local residents could just as easily have collected and sold them, but they did not know how or to whom.

Sometimes, there is an edgier tone to comments about how global change is experienced locally. Reynaldo, who I introduced in Chapter 4, once told me about how he had taken a lot of fresh fish to a fish buyer and was offered 20 pesos per kilogram for the entire lot. The lot, however, included a blue marlin, a variety of fish that commands a higher price when sold separately. Reynaldo asked the buyer to weigh and price the blue marlin separately from his other fish, but the buyer refused, citing standard practice and company rules. Reynaldo acknowledged that

Courtesy of James F. Eder

FIGURE 6.4 Brothers ride the family water buffalo

his blue marlin was small and if the buyer had acceded to his request, it would not have made a big difference in his total payment. He nonetheless felt that he had been cheated. "We're always being nickled and dimed here," he told me. "Rich people take advantage of us so that they can become richer."

Sometimes there are also small acts of resistance, but for the most part these are few and far between. Tony told me of a time that he had become so angry about being "squeezed" by a fish buyer that he took his business elsewhere, even though it cost him money to do so. Tony had brought his fish to a Taiwanese fish buyer who offered him 40 pesos per kilogram for fish that in Tony's view were worth more. Worse, the buyer acted as if he was doing Tony a favor by even offering to buy his fish. Tony refused to sell and as he left he told the buyer, "I'd rather sell to a Filipino for thirty-five than to a Taiwanese for forty" (i.e., Tony felt that if someone was going to profit at his expense, he would rather it be a local resident than an outsider).

GLOBALIZATION IS NOT FAIR

Globalization has created new ways of making money from San Vicente's coastal resources, but for the most part, local people are not the ones making it. Rather, outsiders such as fish pen owners, beach resort operators, and pebble collectors are making the money. Worse, some outsiders like fish buyers are making that money at local expense, and it is not just that most local people are losing out, but that they are being exploited by those who are winning. Within this general pattern, however, lies significant variation, and more is at stake than unfairness. Some local residents have benefited from global forces. Different global forces push and pull in different directions and at times even conflict with one another. For example, women may find some traditional economic activities, such as beach seining, closed off by environmentalist pressures, even as microfinance programs make new economic activities possible. Similarly, globally funded coastal resource management programs ask local fishermen to curtail certain fishing practices held to be environmentally damaging, in the interest of conservation, even as global economic forces encourage and legitimize the spread of fish pens, pearl farms, and other extractive activities, in the interest of economic gain.

7

✴

Household Livelihoods
and Conservation

Previous chapters have documented how global forces have affected natural resources and human lives in San Vicente, often for the worse. Some residents have still managed to get ahead economically, but most are struggling to get by. Although the CRMP enjoyed modest success in its effort to help the municipal government better manage coastal resources, degradation of those resources continues. This chapter reviews what I found out about San Vicente, as I pursued the four research questions that I posed in Chapter 1. Based on my findings, the chapter suggests how the people of San Vicente might be helped to strike a better deal with global change, with respect both to their environment and to their livelihoods.

LOCAL LIVELIHOODS AND PATTERNS
OF RESOURCE USE

My first research task was to determine how the inhabitants of San Vicente used coastal resources to make their livings and how people varied in this regard, within and between communities. Everywhere I found that people earned their livings by fishing or farming or by some combination of the two. I showed in Chapter 4 that "fishing" and "farming" are broad and diverse categories. Fishermen and farmers in San Vicente vary in their ownership of land, fishing boats and gear, and other productive equipment. They also vary in their ethnic backgrounds and personal skills and interests. Some fishermen deploy fishing nets from motorized pumpboats; others fish by hook and line from small outrigger canoes. Similarly, some farmers grow irrigated rice on the coastal plain; others plant corn, root crops, and fruit trees on hillsides. Nonetheless, there is a sameness to San Vicente's ten communities and to coastal communities throughout the

Philippines. Fishing boats and farms exist everywhere. Beneath this apparent sameness, however, lie significant differences. Fishermen do not simply employ different gear, nor do farmers simply plant different crops, for within each of these broad categories people use coastal resources in different ways.

Chapter 5 showed how resource use differences sometimes put local residents at odds with one another regarding how best to manage those resources. Unlike maritime peoples elsewhere in the Pacific, fishermen in the Philippines lack customary systems of marine tenure or other traditional "common property" resource management institutions that can help adjudicate such management conflicts as they arise. In some longer settled coastal areas where in-migration has not clouded the distinction between local residents and outsiders, local residents may share an underlying sense of local resources as common property that belongs more to them than to others (Austin 2003), but for the most part, the ocean in the Philippines is an open-access resource, free to all, and no fisherman has the customary means to prevent others from exploiting any particular resource or fishing ground as they see fit. This is particularly true in San Vicente, where many residents are of migrant origin.

In the Solomon Islands, fishing grounds are not freely accessible. Local, kinship-based groups regulate marine resource use by means of customary, nonformalized regulations and other traditional constraints on individual behavior. Customary marine tenure is a system of social relationships whereby fishermen are entitled to use certain fishing grounds or "estates," to use certain fishing techniques, or to fish for certain species by virtue of their birth into a kinship-based group that controls these entitlements (Aswani 1999; Hviding 1996).

In the Marovo Lagoon of the Solomon Islands, one of the world's largest tropical coral reef lagoons, the traditional entitlements and responsibilities associated with membership in quasi-corporate bilateral kinship groups (*butubutu*) helped foster a "deeply custodial relationship" (Hviding 1996: xiv) between local inhabitants and their marine resources. There are about twenty *butubutu* in all, each responsible for a tract of the seas and the reefs within Marovo lagoon. Each individual is a member of several different *butubutu* and has varying claims on its resources, depending on the nature of his or her kinship ties to that group (Hviding 1996: 143). Each *butubutu* has a diverse set of customary regulations on the activities of both members and outsiders within its traditional marine territory. Most allow subsistence fishing but not commercial fishing by people from other groups. Some *butubutu* prohibit both members and outsiders from using nets on the reefs, on the grounds that nets catch too many fish, whereas others allow nets for subsistence fishing but not for commercial fishing (Hviding 1996: 278–279). *Butubutu* elders also periodically and ceremonially "open" and "shut" various reefs to fishing, or to particular kinds of fishing, in preparation for large feasts or in response to localized over-fishing. Supernaturally sanctioned taboos traditionally enforced the reef closures thus declared, and group leaders rotated closures among taboo and non-taboo reefs to minimize subsistence hardships for group members.

Although customary marine tenure systems are vulnerable to economic and social changes, particularly those associated with global forces (Aswani 1999), they nonetheless provide modern resource managers with a set of traditional understandings about environmental rights and responsibilities upon which to build new programs. San Vicente's residents lacked such traditional understandings.

The superficial "fishing boats and farms" sameness to San Vicente's coastal communities is deceptive in another way, for it might lead a casual observer to conclude that fishing and farming are the only economic activities whereby local people earn their livings. Chapter 4 showed that though most people primarily fish or farm for their livings, many also engage in other economic activities. These supplementary activities, or "sidelines," provide badly needed additional income, especially in fishing households squeezed between declining fish catches and the rising cost of gasoline. Entrepreneurial, risk-taking women figure prominently in the development of supplementary household economic activities, and I showed in Chapter 6 how new microfinance programs today help capitalize these activities.

GLOBAL FORCES AND LOCAL LIVES

My second research question asked how global forces had affected coastal resources and people's lives in San Vicente. I found that global forces had accelerated depletion of local resources and undermined local livelihoods. Chapter 3 showed how powerful outsiders associated with the logging, mining, and commercial fishing industries in the Philippines often elbow aside local "small people" and degrade the environment in their quests for resource-extraction profits. I also have showed in this book that migration from other parts of the Philippines has swelled the numbers of local fishermen and that some employ destructive or illegal fishing techniques. Local people, too, have degraded the environment in their own quests to secure a living. The declining catches of San Vicente fishermen documented in Chapters 4 and 5 reflect this confluence of global and local forces on the municipality's coastal resources.

More is at stake than this "outside exploiters versus local exploiters" rendition of coastal resource use in the Philippines might suggest. Other influences are at work, and they do not all push in the same direction. The openness of the Philippines to global forces of all kinds, not just those connected with resource exploitation, has helped foster a vigorous environmental movement. Global pressures to conserve the nation's remaining biodiversity have led to many programs to better manage coastal resources, including the ambitious Coastal Resource Management Project (CRMP), discussed in Chapter 5. Earlier, I explained how the Philippines lacks the potentially useful building blocks of customary marine tenure systems and well-developed local norms of fishing behavior. Government agencies and nongovernmental organizations (NGOs) must instead help local residents to build new resource management systems from the ground up. Chapter 3 showed, however, that the government has a poor track record in resource management and has long encouraged or legitimized unsustainable resource extraction by political allies, economic elites, and other outsiders. For this reason, many rural dwellers view with suspicion all outside interventions aimed at resource conservation.

An important finding of Chapter 4 was that not all local "small people" experience or respond to global forces equally. Some San Vicente residents are doing better than others economically. Many have been squeezed by global changes and feel they are losing out, whereas others have taken advantage of those same changes to survive and even to prosper. Some rural Filipinos appear resilient and even entrepreneurial in the face of change, whereas others seem exploited or left out. This observation informed my earlier dissertation research, in a farming community near Puerto Princesa City, and ultimately led to writing a book with the title, *Who Shall Succeed?* There I explored the role that such factors as prior geographical mobility, husband-wife "chemistry" (as I called it at the time), and even luck played in determining why some migrants to the frontier did better economically than others, despite seeming "equal opportunity" (Eder 1982). In San Vicente, I might recast "equal opportunity" as "equal adversity." Without claiming that the residents of San Vicente are all equally energetic, resilient, or entrepreneurial, however, my position is that many of those who are not currently prospering have the energy and ability needed to do so if conditions were different.

TOWARD MORE EFFECTIVE COASTAL RESOURCE MANAGEMENT

My third research question concerned the CRMP's effort to relieve exploitative pressures on coastal resources and manage those resources on a more sustainable basis. Why did the project not accomplish more during its 6 years in San Vicente, and how might things have been done differently? A growing academic literature considers the successes and failures of coastal resource management projects in the Philippines and elsewhere (see, e.g., Christie et al. 1994; Pollnac, Crawford, and Gorospe 2001; Pomeroy and Pido 1995; Pomeroy et al. 2005; Sunderlin and Gorospe 1997; and White, Courtney, and Salamanca 2002). Particularly helpful is a recent study that compares forty-five community-based marine protected areas (MPAs) in the Visayan Islands region of the Philippines. The authors of this comparative study sought to determine what attributes the more successful protected areas had in common, with the aim of identifying "predictors" of likely project success elsewhere (Pollnac et al. 2001). Of the forty-five protected areas considered in the study, some existed only in legislation or were not functional, but others had achieved considerable success.

Among the latter was a MPA on Apo Island, one of the first and most successful in the Philippines (Alcala 2001). Located near Negros Island in the Visayas, Apo Island was the site of a resource conservation project initiated in 1979 by social and marine scientists from nearby Silliman University. Following a lengthy campaign to educate local fishing people about environmental issues and to equip them with the needed management skills, university scientists worked with local authorities to establish an 11-hectare protected area in 1984. Several years elapsed before many local residents embraced the project, but fishermen who initially objected to the protected area concept today willingly cooperate with other local residents to defend their MPA from illegal fishing activities.

A second generation of local residents is now assuming control of the Apo Island project, which has attracted worldwide attention for its accomplishments in combining marine conservation, ecotourism, and sustainable livelihood development. A local tourist business maintains a website that includes a brief history of the project and a discussion of current conservation challenges (http://www. apoisland.com/), and a short Greenpeace video celebrates the Apo Island MPA as a model to be emulated elsewhere in the world (http://tvyil.greenpeaceweb.org/default.asp?loadcat=17).

For every Apo Island in the Philippines, however, there have been numerous failures, and only about 20 to 25 percent of the nation's more than 400 MPAs have been successful (Pollnac et al. 2001: 684). What, precisely, constitutes "success" in a MPA? Richard Pollnac and his colleagues began their analysis by establishing five measurable indicators of protected area success. These measures included increases in the quality and quantity of fish; community members' perception of the protected area's impact on fish stocks; establishment and maintenance of a management plan, marker buoys, and a management committee; degree of adherence to the rules; and the empowering of community residents to manage their own resources (Pollnac et al 2001: 684–685). Next, the authors analyzed the strength of the correlations between these success measures and a series of independent variables, some location-specific (such as community population size) and others intrinsic to the project itself (such as financial inputs and the presence of a live-in extension worker). Based on this analysis, the authors concluded that of all the variables considered, six were particularly important to MPA success: a relatively small population size; a preexisting, perceived crisis related to reduced fish populations; successful alternative income projects; a relatively high level of community participation in decision making; continuing advice from the implementing organization; and inputs from the municipal government (Pollnac et al. 2001: 706–707).

How might the CRMP in San Vicente be evaluated on these six predictors of MPA success? Only for two predictors, a prior perceived crisis in fish stocks and inputs from the municipal government, would San Vicente rank high. For the other four success predictors, San Vicente would rank low when compared with the projects considered in the study. Here, I will further discuss one of the other four success predictors: a relatively high level of community participation in decision making. The authors of another recent comparative study of coastal resource management projects also emphasize this factor:

> Participation of community members in . . . project design and implementation and real or perceived economic benefits from the project influence participants to sustain project activities after project completion. This should come as no surprise. Participation in project design and implementation provides community members with a sense of "ownership" over the project. Since the community members helped to create the . . . project, it provides a greater probability that aspects of the project fit the needs of community members. (Pomeroy et al. 2005: 375)

The notion that projects to better manage natural resources require the active participation of local residents is today widely accepted as a policy goal. If local residents are to assume ownership and manage such projects successfully after the implementing agency departs, they need to participate from the start. Resource users who feel they are not consulted or do not participate meaningfully in the process whereby MPAs are established are less willing later to honor the terms of the arrangement, and they are more likely to turn to subtle forms of resistance and even to sabotage. Chapter 5 showed how failure to negotiate satisfactorily at the outset where protected areas would be located and what the terms of their use would be came back later to haunt the CRMP. Resistors stole marker buoys, and many fishermen did not feel obligated to honor MPA boundaries or rules.

Meaningful local participation is easy to call for, but it often goes unrealized in practice. Attention to the nature of "participation" itself helps explain why. First, there is an important subjective dimension to the notion, and second, there are different kinds of participation. The subjective aspects of participation emerged in conversations I had in San Vicente with fishermen who claimed that they had not participated in the decision-making process, even though the process was ostensibly participatory and included various local community meetings. Thus, regarding the process that led to the selection of the MPAs discussed in Chapter 5, fishermen who relied on oar rather than on motor power did not simply feel that they had lost out; they felt that their voices and concerns had not received fair hearing.

I explained in Chapter 5 that these community meetings occurred before my field research, but based on subsequent interviews with a variety of attendees with different involvements and perspectives on the CRMP, I found that the meetings were only weakly participatory. Project and local government officials listened to the viewpoints and opinions expressed by community members, but some of the policies later announced and implemented were not based on a community consensus about how best to proceed. This aspect of the conduct of the meetings later gave rise to the numerous complaints that local residents had not really participated in the larger process, even if they had attended the meetings. Furthermore, few of the economically marginal men and women, such as those involved in beach seining, even attended the meetings. In the rural Philippines, such social differences as class and gender often shape or restrict collective action by excluding the poor and particularly poor women from formal community discussions.

Bina Agarwal discusses the different forms that participation by women takes in community meetings about forest management projects in different parts of India and Nepal. In most projects, she observed or learned that women's participation was "nominal" or "passive." Women who attended community meetings did not speak or, if they did speak, they did not express their own views or challenge authority. "What is the point of going to meetings," one woman in a village community told Agarwal, "we would just sit silently." Another said, "I attend (the) meetings, but I only sign. I don't say much or I say I agree" (Agarwal 2001: 1628). Agarwal contrasts these kinds of participation with "active" and (ultimately) "empowering" participation, where participants express opinions whether or not they are solicited, take initiatives of other kinds, and influence the group's decisions. In those rare cases where women participated in community forestry meetings in more active and meaningful ways, Agarwal found that they sometimes came up with more suitable alternatives than the men had regarding such matters as when grass should be cut or which trees should be planted. She concludes that more meaningful inclusion of women in community forestry projects in India and Nepal would lead to greater efficiencies in forest protection and to better community reforestation decisions (Agarwal 2001).

To achieve success, resource managers need to strive for active and empowering participation by all local residents to build community consensus and to help ensure better resource management outcomes. Local participation in the CRMP was only of the nominal or passive kind, especially by women and the poor. Peter Utting aptly characterizes such simplistic models of consultation and dialogue often associated with community-based conservation programs as "technocratic participation" for their failure to adequately engage broader community interests and the views and priorities of weaker social groups (2000: 194).

One way to ensure that community meetings are more inclusive and that a greater variety of local perspectives are represented is through the creation of new institutional arrangements (Agrawal and Gibson 2001) or what S. Jentoft and colleagues (1998: 427) call "changing the rules." An emphasis on institutions focuses on the ability of communities to create and to enforce those rules. However, the issue is not so much the rules as it is the communicative and collaborative process through which the rules are formed: who participates, how to structure debates, how to address conflicts of interest, and how to reach agreements (Jentoft et al. 1998: 427). The CRMP worked primarily within the existing institutional environment. In its carefully crafted "PRO-CRM" plan to guide future coastal resource management efforts following project termination, project managers made a virtue of turning their responsibilities over to a crowded suite of existing municipal and provincial government and private agencies and programs, a virtual roll call of established political and social groupings in Palawan. In addition to the bureaucratic obstacles presented by such an unwieldy arrangement, it also guaranteed that the existing institutional inequities in wider Philippine society would continue to be projected onto local development. San Vicente's experience with the CRMP is consistent with the general observations of David Natcher and Clifford Hickey about such programs:

> Despite enhanced local involvement in resource management, final decisions often remain reflective of only the dominant modes of prevailing power at the time, thereby muting alternative perspectives, insights, and systems of knowing. Consequently, by failing to account for community pluralism, local efforts all too often only soften the traditional top-down relationship long inherent in resource management, resulting in the continued subjugation of values and concerns of some community members. (2002: 351)

An adequate accounting of community pluralism and effective local governance of coastal resources are unlikely to result from a one-time community meeting where project organizers discuss the terms of a particular local governance project, such as a MPA, and then move on. Rather, local governance is a process that needs ongoing facilitation and support by deliberation and inclusion

(Renard 2005; Utting 2000). Project managers may object that such a process is too costly and time-consuming. "We can't afford to do that," a CRMP staff member told me, when I delicately suggested that the project should have made greater effort in particular local communities to work through the MPA establishment process with various local resource users; "We're a big project and we work in a lot of different communities." Without broad-based local participation, however, the outcome may be projects that exist only on paper or collapse after project funding and external assistance cease to be available.

In the real world of most coastal fishing communities, resource management project success might appear be out of reach, but Pollnac and his colleagues found other successful projects in the Philippines besides the one at Apo Island, and other researchers have found successful projects elsewhere in the world. In the island nation of Saint Lucia, located in the Windward Islands in the eastern Caribbean, many local inhabitants depend on coastal resources for their livelihoods in much the same way as the inhabitants of San Vicente do. For 3 years, Yves Renard studied the efforts of Saint Lucia's residents to better manage their coastal resources (Renard 2005). These resources include beaches, coral reefs, sea grass beds, and small mangroves. Most coastal residents, particularly the poorer ones, depend largely or even entirely on various forms of fishing and on harvesting sea urchins and wild seaweed. As in San Vicente, coastal resources in Saint Lucia support multiple livelihood activities, and some local residents also farm on the coastal plain or find part-time employment in the tourist economy. Also, population increase and a history of ineffective resource management efforts have led to serious environmental issues: pollution, habitat degradation and destruction, and depletion of fish stocks (Renard 2005: 161–162).

Renard conducted his research in Saint Lucia in Laborie, a fishing community with a population of about 5,000 people. Because of declining global demand for Saint Lucia's agricultural exports, residents of Laborie who once earned part of their livings by growing bananas had increased pressure on marine resources to sustain themselves. As the national economy declined, local poverty levels grew. Some people emigrated abroad or sought employment in Saint Lucia's tourist industry, but most remained in Laborie. In a national political system based on patronage and favoritism, many community members felt marginalized and excluded from the benefits of government-sponsored development projects ostensibly aimed at improving the economic picture (Renard 2005: 163). In a turn for the better in 1999, a diverse group of 25 local leaders dissatisfied with the dominant approach to development constituted themselves as the Laborie Development Planning Committee. With the support of a national government agency (the Department of Fisheries) and a regional NGO (The Caribbean Natural Resources Institute), and after 2 years of extensive local research and consultation that included sector workshops, focus group sessions, and informal discussions, the committee formulated a strategic development plan for Laborie (Renard 2005: 163–164).

This plan emphasized coastal resource management and the relationship between resource management and social and economic development, including poverty reduction. While the committee finalized the plan, the same outside agencies that had helped the community to prepare it embarked on a 3-year research project to identify and help implement the specific institutional arrangements best suited to local governance of the plan's proposed resource management and livelihood development activities. These activities included managing the sea urchin fishery, seaweed farming, community-based tourism, and promoting awareness of pollution. For all four activities, the local development planning committee responded proactively to local needs, such as product development and marketing assistance. The committee also placed great emphasis on participatory procedures, including community meetings for expressing and reconciling diverse viewpoints, and on protecting the rights and interests of the poor. With respect to managing the sea urchin fishery, for example, Laborie residents disagreed about the matter of access rights. Younger harvesters advocated formal rules to guarantee to local residents exclusive rights to nearby stocks. More experienced sea urchin harvesters and local residents who exploited other marine resources worried that such exclusion would cause people in other communities to retaliate and prevent access to fisheries of other kinds. After what Renard describes as a "heated and difficult debate," all parties agreed that formal exclusion was not possible but that certain informal steps would ensure that local harvesters had priority access to local stocks (Renard 2005: 168).

The results of the Laborie project lasted beyond the life of the project and include an institutionalized partnership between state agencies and local resource users, acceptance of the use of both local and scientific knowledge in deciding how best to manage the sea urchin fishery, improved marketing arrangements, and greater community control over resource access and use (Renard 2005: 169). Renard draws two lessons from his case study. First, it shows that local empowerment in natural resource governance can happen, and that it can have positive impacts on livelihood and poverty reduction. Second, natural resource management, especially in a coastal context, requires an integrated and functional system of local governance that incorporates a variety of actors and processes, including government agencies (Renard 2005: 152–153). The commitments by all involved to achieving genuine local participation, to making local governance work, and to addressing the livelihood concerns of local residents, particularly the poorer ones, are all important reasons for the success of this coastal resource management and development planning initiative in Saint Lucia.

Might coastal resource management projects achieve similar success in Palawan? At least one already has. In 2004, residents of the community of Caramay, located in the municipality of Roxas opposite San Vicente on the east coast of Palawan, established a large marine sanctuary. Their project involved a partnership between local resource users and the municipal government, but with external financial support from the Royal Netherlands Embassy in the Philippines and the United Nations Development Programme (UNDP). I was unable to visit this project myself, but upon hearing that it was widely considered a great success, I sought out officials in the Bureau of Fisheries and at the Palawan Council of Sustainable Development (PCSD) who were familiar with the Caramay project (and also with the CRMP in San Vicente) to learn why. I found that external financial support was important, but the key to the project's success was that a local people's organization, the "Small Fishermen of Caramay Producers Cooperative," had taken the initiative in establishing and operating the sanctuary. "They own it," said the head of the Bureau of Fisheries office, but they only became ready for such ownership following 6 years of gradual community "preparation" that had occurred in conjunction with another resource management project, implemented by an environmentalist NGO in Puerto Princesa City.

Another important ingredient of the Caramay project was that local residents received training in surveillance against intrusion and monitoring of the recovery of fish stocks, both crucial to MPA success (Newkirk and Rivera 1996). In San Vicente, according to the PCSD official, the CRMP never "capacitated" local residents and instead simply left them and an unprepared municipal government to "figure it out on their own." At Caramay, local residents used project funds to construct a floating monitoring station adjacent to the new sanctuary. Here local fishermen take turns with guard duty following procedures learned in a workshop sponsored by a fisheries expert from the provincial government. They periodically collect data to document the recovery of local fish stocks. The Fisheries Office reported that these stocks were indeed recovering, although I did not see any documentation myself. More recently, managers have added an ecotourism component to the project with an eye toward diversifying local livelihoods. Tourists can hire boats from local fishermen and, after paying a small "environmental fee," see the marine sanctuary firsthand. The fee proceeds pay for project operations.

UNDP phased out its support for the project at Caramay in early 2006, and local residents began to operate the sanctuary independently. Though still facing uncertainties, the project demonstrates that with strategically implemented outside assistance, local residents are capable of developing and maintaining new and more effective resource management institutions. In June 2006 and following a Palawan-wide competition, the Caramay marine sanctuary and livelihood support project received the Governor's Award for Environmental Protection.

Based on my reading of these and other comparative success cases from near and far and on my own findings about local responses to the CRMP in San Vicente, here are my recommendations to those who would implement other such projects in the Philippines. Similar recommendations made before have yet to be considered or widely implemented.

First, project managers should work harder to develop local participation and project ownership. They should recognize that effective local governance is a process that will only develop over time if supported by deliberation and inclusion. To that end, significant compromises with local residents may be necessary and appropriate. With respect to proposals to establish MPAs, project managers may need to compromise with local community members regarding the severity of restrictions on entering or fishing in such areas. Instead of declaring them to be "no-take" zones as favored by environmentalists, and as attempted in San Vicente, project managers might establish multipurpose protected areas allowing limited access using less destructive gear types. This kind of compromise has helped mobilize local support for MPAs in the Bahamas (Stouffle and Minnis 2005) and on various Pacific Islands (Gilman 1997). I believe that a similar compromise with local residents in favor of limited-access rather than no-take zoning of environmentally important coastal habitats would prove beneficial to the overall coastal resource management effort in the Philippines. Despite less protection on paper, more conservation would occur in practice because local residents would be more supportive of individual projects. The emphasis on "capacity building" currently popular with government agencies and NGOs also promises to facilitate greater local support and ownership of resource management projects, but time will tell if the "capacity" in question will be only to administer programs that others have designed. To develop the capacity to secure outside support for projects that are locally designed and best serve local interests will require, among other things, confronting the inequities in the nation's wider political economy discussed in Chapter 3.

Second, project managers should carefully consider whether a MPA is a necessary or appropriate strategy in a particular area. MPAs may not be the best choice everywhere. According to Renard, the biological diversity and other conditions of some coastal areas of Saint Lucia did not warrant MPAs and called for other management strategies (Renard 2005: 165–166). Although the biological diversity of coastal Palawan warrants MPAs, my findings suggest that its social diversity may be such that in some places local residents may be unable to agree or compromise on their value and rules of use. In such places, efforts to establish MPAs may undermine other and potentially more rewarding attempts at local collective action on behalf of conservation. Caramay is located in a long-settled and ethnically relatively homogeneous part of Palawan, and that contributes to the apparent success of the protected area there. Elsewhere in Palawan where local residents differ in ethnic background and gear type as much as they do in San Vicente, it may be premature and too much of an uphill battle to attempt to establish a viable system of MPAs. Certainly the 20 to 25 percent success rate of MPAs in the Philippines cited earlier suggests that projects should pay careful attention to whether the factors that determine protected area success or failure are in place.

Third, coastal resource project managers need to give proportionately greater attention to livelihood issues than they do at present. To relieve pressure on fish stocks, one of the most effective measures may be to devote more effort and resources to developing new livelihoods for fishing households. This strategy may be particularly useful in coastal areas such as San Vicente, where local residents want more control over their lives and resources, rather than a "list of don'ts," as one skeptical fisherman characterized the CRMP agenda to me. Reflecting on the project he studied in Saint Lucia, Renard reached a similar conclusion:

> Dominant approaches in coastal resource management, in the Caribbean as in many other parts of the developing world, are concerned primarily with resource conservation, resource use control and conflict management. One of the lessons of this project is that local institutional arrangements need to give far greater attention to economic aspects, with a focus on poverty reduction and equity issues (Renard 2005: 175).

In short, the managers of resource projects need to rethink their perceptions of local livelihoods. The CRMP itself agreed with this proposition in its own completion report. According to this report, among the major lessons learned from the project's experience was that coastal resource management programs needed to directly address poverty issues:

> The argument that CRM will in the long term provide greater economic benefits to resource users than current unsustainable practices is lame against the backdrop of hand-to-mouth poverty. Marginal fishers who are asked to stop destructive fishing must be assured of livelihood assistance that will allow them to "survive" low yields and income for as long as it takes fishery stocks and habitats to recover their productivity.... (CRMP 2004: 111)

COASTAL ZONE LIVELIHOODS FOR
THE TWENTY-FIRST CENTURY

My fourth question followed from my third and asked what anthropology could contribute to identifying these needed new livelihoods. I answer this question in two ways. First, I draw on my observations of San Vicente's coastal economy and of the more economically successful households to suggest two important criteria that new livelihoods should meet. Second, I draw on comparative studies of new economic activities that meet these criteria and have demonstrated substantial promise in other coastal areas, to suggest specific new livelihood possibilities appropriate for San Vicente.

One of my main ethnographic findings in Chapter 4 was that most households in San Vicente depend on multiple sources of income, whether their primary occupation is fishing or farming. Households in the coastal zone are accustomed to exploiting different economic activities simultaneously and in ways that involve a complex interdependence of the labor of husband and wife. Writing of development options for the coastal zones of Southeast Asia, Conner Bailey and Caroline Pomeroy see considerable virtue in this circumstance:

> Fishing communities in Southeast Asia are dependent upon a complex coastal ecosystem, not simply any one component. Fishers and members of their families occupy multiple niches and utilize a diversity of resources. This occupational multiplicity provides coastal communities with a significant degree of economic and social stability. (1996: 196)

In San Vicente, Bailey and Pomeroy's view that household economies in the coastal zone are "based on a wide range of income sources that are widely distributed both temporally and spatially" and are "dependent not on a single resource but on a whole ecosystem" (1996: 195) does not apply equally to all households. I also showed in Chapter 4 that some households are entirely dependent on fishing and, hence, on a single, diminishing resource. Nonetheless, I find Bailey and Pomeroy's emphasis attractive and consistent with my own findings that occupational diversity is a socially and economically healthy phenomenon that takes advantage of the natural diversity found in tropical coastal zones (1996: 196).

Their observations help frame two important criteria to guide efforts to strengthen this desirable economic diversification and hence build household and community stability and prosperity.

First, to be economically attractive to local residents, new livelihoods must be integrated vertically and laterally with both the local economy and the global economy. New livelihoods must relate in identifiable and predictable ways with available resources, sources of information, marketing channels, and local or external market demand. New livelihoods must also fit with the cash and capital-short circumstances of most rural residents and with the availability and cost of labor, within and beyond the household. These and other kinds of integration are essential if the local adopters of proposed new livelihoods can continue to pursue them over the long term, after project sponsors leave (Pomeroy, Parks, and Balboa 2006: 127).

In Chapter 4, I presented several cases of entrepreneurial households whose members had developed new livelihoods and had achieved, or begun to achieve, this needed integration. In the process, each of these households improved its economic circumstances. One case involved Remy's snack food business, which drew on the subsistence resources of her husband Ramon's upland farm to meet the demand of high school students in a neighboring community for fresh between-meal snacks. Other cases presented in Chapter 4 concerned Lando and Gina's dried fish-making business and Peter and Rachel's buy-and-sell business. Both operations successfully integrated household and other local labor resources with existing sources of supply to expand on or profit from already-present market links. In contrast, Edna's silkworm-raising effort and Nicanor's monitor lizard venture, also discussed in Chapter 4, were not well integrated vertically or laterally and they never really got off the ground because they were based on incomplete information and uncertain market links.

The lesson here is that the development of new rural livelihoods is as much a matter of developing marketing channels and providing local residents with access to strategic information on prices and markets as it is a matter of technical assistance about how to raise silkworms or to grow seaweed. Without access to such strategic information, local residents are often unable to tell whether a particular new activity, such as silkworm culture or seaweed farming, has only limited potential or is an opportunity for expansion open to all. I showed in Chapter 6 how microfinance programs have been an important source of starting capital for new economic activities in San Vicente, but unfortunately these programs often fail to provide the training, market access, and other nonfinancial services that poor women need to make effective use of their micro-loans (Harper 2005: 6–7).

Lynne Milgram studied a microfinance program aimed at craftswomen in Banaue, in Ifugao Province in the northern Philippines, intended to alleviate poverty by increasing women's employment. This program operated in much the same way as the two microfinance programs in San Vicente described in Chapter 6. Woodcarvings produced by the Ifugao residents of Banaue are popular with domestic and foreign tourists, and many local women took out loans to begin or expand woodcarving or other handicraft businesses. Other women took out loans to open or expand small grocery stores. The microfinance program, however, did not take adequate account of the wider social system within which women's economic activities occur and in particular the economic infrastructure in which most female entrepreneurs operate. According to Milgram,

> Craftswomen in Banaue ... receive financial support for production (raw materials), but do not receive assistance to develop broader socioeconomic linkages that would provide consultation on competitive product design, access to urban markets, and social support networks (e.g., child care, health care). (2001: 220)

The result was that the loan program primarily served the needs of women with established businesses. They were already knowledgeable about market opportunities and market channels, and they could more easily meet the program's stringent weekly repayment schedule. Some women in this category used loans to purchase additional stock for already-existing grocery or craft stores. One such woman, Rosa, operated a small craft store in the town market and traveled each month to Manila to sell her products. She used her loan to purchase additional wood and rattan for her craft producers and to open a small grocery store in her house (Milgram 2001: 219). In contrast, poorer women, who might have benefited most from the loans and at whom the microfinance program was ostensibly aimed, were reluctant to participate. Most of those poorer women who did take out loans fell behind on repayments because they could not achieve financial self-sustainability fast enough to meet program expectations. Women who took out loans to open stores found that the loans were too small to allow them to purchase adequate initial stock or to ensure the cash flow required to meet the loan repayment schedule. Women who borrowed money to produce crafts or to purchase and raise pigs struggled to meet pay their weekly loan repayments while their pigs matured or while they looked for buyers for their crafts (Milgram 2001: 219).

Rather than empowering poor women or lifting them out of poverty, the loan program in Ifugao reinforced preexisting class differences between poor and better-off women (Milgram 2005: 220). Milgram's observations resonate with my own in San Vicente and suggest the need for more effective state-local and NGO-local collaboration to develop additional support for entrepreneurs and would-be entrepreneurs, new household livelihoods, and rural economic growth. Such collaboration can help those who struggle with establishing broader socioeconomic linkages and experience poor results.

A second criterion that new coastal zone livelihoods should meet is that they be the occupations not just of individuals but the activities of households, both to draw on the combined energies and skills of husband and wife and to relieve pressures on natural resources. This criterion emerged from my observations of households in San Vicente that had responded most successfully to the challenges and opportunities posed by global change. The just-discussed household enterprises of Peter and Rachel, Lando and Gina, and Remy and Ramon meet this criterion as well. Each of these households is more prosperous than it was before when husband and wife worked at separate activities. Other households in San Vicente are in the process of moving to this model of lateral economic integration within the household and appear poised to become more prosperous. If Sylvia's canteen business (Chapter 6) continues to grow and she can convince her husband to stop fishing and instead raise pigs to supply her canteen with fresh pork, or if Russielle's hog-raising enterprise (Chapter 4) expands to the point that Bruce Lee will give up fishing in favor of cultivating feed corn and manioc, both households will likely be better off than they are today and place less pressure on local fish stocks.

These observations suggest that economic diversification through household enterprise development may have a more beneficial effect on coastal economies and resources than will the provision of "alternative" livelihoods that offer employment to individual members of households but do not change a household's primary subsistence strategy. Household enterprise development may be particularly beneficial to coastal communities such as those in San Vicente where fishing is largely the domain of men and most newly-proposed livelihood activities are for women. Periodic employment in one of San Vicente's two sardine factories may be important to some local women, but such work does not constitute an alternative livelihood so much as it does a supplementary one (see Crawford 2002). To the degree that the husbands of these factory-working women continue to fish as before, such supplementary employment does little to relieve exploitation pressures on coastal resources. In contrast, where the supplementary economic activities of women become genuine household enterprises harnessing women's labor, technical skills, and economic planning abilities for the benefit of the entire household, there is the potential to relieve exploitative pressures on fish stocks.

What are some specific new livelihoods that meet these two criteria? Seaweed farming remains a possibility. As I showed in Chapter 5, seaweed farming can employ the labor of several household members, and it fits well with other household economic activities. It connects laterally to local resources and vertically to world market demand, although the needed market links in San Vicente are still in progress. Seaweed farming started in San Vicente 10 years ago. Today only about thirty households are involved in this activity, suggesting that it does not fully meet these criteria or does not pay well enough to attract other growers.

Two further livelihood possibilities for San Vicente are sustainable aquaculture and community-based tourism. Aquaculture is the cultivation of fish, shellfish, and other aquatic organisms. It differs from fishing in that the goal is to maintain or increase the number of organisms involved, rather than simply capturing them from the ocean. The fish pens used to raise grouper and wrasses for the live fish trade are an example of aquaculture. As I showed in Chapter 3, the live fish trade is not presently a sustainable form of aquaculture because of the widespread use of cyanide to obtain the juvenile fish in the wild. Marine scientists in Indonesia and elsewhere in the Pacific are currently studying ways to propagate in hatcheries the juvenile fish needed to stock fish pens, reasoning that if these and other coral reef organisms increase in number, pressures on wild stocks will diminish. Furthermore, small-scale aquaculture of these and other coral reef organisms may provide a technologically feasible and economically appealing alternative livelihood for fishing households that would otherwise continue to exploit wild fish stocks (Pomeroy et al. 2006: 112–113).

Since 1998 in Bali, a marine research institute with funding from the Indonesian and Canadian governments has promoted a "Backyard Multi-species Hatchery System" whereby local households can engage in "seed production" of grouper and other species later raised to adulthood in fish pens. Many technical, economic, and environmental issues remain to be resolved, but today about 2,000 backyard fish hatcheries in Bali employ several household members each on a part- or full-time basis, and they have significantly reduced pressures on wild stocks of these fish (STREAM 2003). I believe that with suitable outside support, this kind of aquaculture would be economically attractive to many San Vicente fishing households. Other kinds of household-based, environmentally friendly aquaculture that might work well in San Vicente include sea cucumber farming and mud crab culture, the latter in small mangrove areas enclosed by bamboo fences in the intertidal zone (Kühlmann 2002).

Community-based tourism aims to ensure that the economic benefits of tourism development are broadly shared among the local residents of the host communities. The small beach resorts that presently ring Port Barton Bay, discussed in Chapter 3, are in some ways community based. Although foreigners own several of them, all provide employment opportunities for local residents. Some local women, like Anecia, whom I introduced in Chapter 4, work at the resorts as cooks or housekeepers, and some local men guide tourists on swimming and diving visits to nearby islands and reefs. Difficulty of transportation access is the principal constraint on further tourism development in San Vicente, but as access improves with better roads and more comfortable vehicles, the numbers of tourists to the municipality will increase, and tourist services and accommodations will begin to appear in other communities besides Port Barton.

Until now, tourism in San Vicente has been community-based largely by default. The municipality is sufficiently off the beaten track and receives so few annual visitors that it has not attracted attention from investors and companies aiming to establish large, high-end resorts that cater to a wealthier clientele. However, change may be on the way. As I mentioned in Chapter 3, one current proposal is to construct a private airport and a five-star resort near Port Barton. Such a resort might become popular with tourists and make a lot of money for its owners but would not likely be as well rooted in the local community as Port Barton's present resorts are. A high-end resort would likely staff most positions with college-educated workers brought in from Manila and elsewhere and would only employ local residents for menial jobs. Local residents would benefit from the spread of small-scale tourist operations to other local communities in addition to Port Barton, operations that would develop local roots by dialoguing with local residents about what kinds of tourism-related activities could be developed and operated by community members.

One such possibility might be ecotourism. Some local fishermen already host tourist visits to mangrove forests and waterfalls, and they could extend these visits to include MPAs, as in Caramay. Another possibility might be home stays, an adaptation of the "bed and breakfast" model whereby the more socially adventuresome tourists take the opportunity to spend a day or even a night with a local family. These are my own ideas about what might work well as tourism develops further in San Vicente. Local residents will likely have better and more practical ideas. My point here is that large, high-end resorts typically do not engage in local dialogue, which is a cornerstone of community-based tourism and essential if host communities are to benefit economically from tourism and tourism is to be socially sustainable locally (Din 1993).

LOOKING AHEAD

Can the Philippines still protect its remaining coastal resources and develop new livelihoods for its millions of coastal zone residents? Pessimism reigns when specialists in the Philippines meet and discuss recent developments and where the country might be headed in the future. When I participate in such discussions myself, and compare my own observations with those of my social science colleagues, I sometimes find myself drawn into a verbal competition to see who can paint the dreariest picture of life in the Philippines or tell the latest or best story about official corruption or environmental despoliation. In this book, I have presented elements of such images, of what life in the Philippines is like. Corruption, in particular, among some politicians and government officials remains a serious problem.

Yet, I am cautiously optimistic about the future. At all levels of the Philippine state, government agencies charged with natural resource management have made substantial progress in dealing with resource management issues. The projects and programs that these agencies are presently implementing, sometimes on their own and sometimes with the support of NGOs and other outside organizations, are more technically sophisticated and more environmentally and socially sound today than in the past. The individuals who implement and staff these projects and programs are better prepared professionally and more committed to project success than are their counterparts in years past. As a visiting social scientist, I had no direct knowledge of corruption, nor could I appropriately investigate allegations or rumors of corruption without risking loss of cooperation with government officials and agencies or otherwise jeopardizing my research and legal status in the country. My own view is that sweeping generalizations about the alleged intentions and honesty of government officials, while fashionable both locally and internationally, are unfair. Although some officials may be dishonest, others—perhaps even most—are not. In my own fieldwork in San Vicente and elsewhere on Palawan, I regularly met politicians and government employees who are professional, knowledgeable, and dedicated to conserving the nation's remaining natural resources and to making the Philippines a better place for all to live.

The significant accomplishments at Apo Island and Caramay show that when conditions are right, ordinary local residents, rather than just the trained staff members of government agencies or nongovernmental organizations, can also rise to the occasion and do their share. I mentioned in Chapter 3 how millions of Filipinos have grown cynical about the abilities and intentions of their government, but they also want their government to work properly and effectively. Where natural resource management programs meet local needs and expectations, local residents continue to cooperate with project managers for the greater good. They are also prepared to take action on their own. One day in San Vicente I accompanied Carlito, a local fisherman, to empty his fish corral of the day's catch. Mixed in with all the fish was a large sea turtle. After I had duly taken a photograph, Carlito released it back into the sea. Sea turtles are an endangered species, he told me, and "We don't eat them anymore," although in the past people always ate sea turtles and still consider them to be a tasty food. A less charitable observer might have concluded that Carlito only released the turtle because I was present, either because he wanted to impress me with his environmental ethic or feared I would tell others if he kept and ate it. I firmly believe that Carlito released the turtle because it had become for him the right thing to do.

Good intentions and concerns for the environment and for the well-being of future generations are important, but they are not enough. Government officials, resource managers, and local residents all need detailed and accurate knowledge to act on those intentions and concerns. Here anthropologists, with our characteristic focus on local social and cultural context, have much to contribute. Our focus enables us to engage and clarify the importance of local-level social processes that others might miss or consider unimportant. In my own research, local engagement paid off with an enhanced understanding of household economic life in San Vicente. This understanding became the basis for my recommendations about what kinds of new livelihoods would best mobilize the energies and skills of women and lead to the development of productive household enterprises.

Focusing on local context also enables anthropologists to explain how cultural differences may undermine community-based resource management programs and to suggest alternative courses of action. My ability to relate the differences in gear types and fishing techniques I observed to broader differences in ethnic background informed my understanding of why the CRMP failed. This understanding led to my recommendation that in places like San Vicente, cultural differences between fishermen are such that limited-take marine reserves would likely lead to better conservation outcomes in the end than would no-take zones. Finally, because anthropologists study the global as well as the local, we are uniquely positioned to understand the many ways that global forces affect the local communities and people that we study. Acting on these understandings, anthropologists can help local people to better voice their concerns and to formulate more effective plans to deal with local problems. I hope that this book will contribute to these important ends.

Appendix A

✳

Common Fish, Mangroves, and Sea Grasses in San Vicente

Fish

Local name	Common English name
alumahan	long-jawed mackerel
anay-anay	giant basslet
asohos	whiting
bakoko	sweetlip
banak	mullet
bangsi	flying fish
bangus	milkfish
bisugo	threadfin bream
burao	mackerel
dalagang bukid	yellow-tailed fusilier
danggit	rabbitfish
dapa	tongue sole
darag-darag	gray snapper
dilis	anchovy
espada	cutlassfish
galunggong	round scad
hasa-hasa	short-bodied mackerel
hilo	eel

(Continued)

Local name	Common English name
kabayo-kabayo	seahorse
kalapato	hunchback trevally
kalaso	lizardfish
kanuping	emperor bream
lapu-lapu	grouper
liwit	hairtail
Vmaming	wrasse
matambaka	big-eyed scad
maya-maya	red snapper
mulmol	parrotfish
pagi	stingray
pak-an	hard-tailed scad
palata	damselfish
pating	shark
rompe	barracuda
salayginto	yellow-striped crevalle
salay-salay	smooth-tailed trevally
salimburao	Indian mackerel
salmollete	goatfish
sapsap	slipmouth; ponyfish
sulid	fusilier
suno	grouper
talakitok	jack
tambakol	skipjack tuna
tamban	sardine
tanguingue	Spanish mackerel
torsillo	seapike
tulingan	frigate tuna

Mangroves

Aegiceras floridum
Bruguiera cylindrical
Bruguiera gymnorrhiza
Ceriops tagal
Rhizophora apiculata
Rhizophora mucronata
Sonneratia alba
Xylocarpus granatum
Xylocarpus moluccencis

Sea Grasses

Cymodocea rotundata
Cymodocea serrulata
Enhalus acoroides
Halophila ovalis
Halodule pinifolia
Halodule uninervis
Syringodium isoetifolium
Thalassia hemipprichii

SOURCES: Arquiza 1999; Austin 2003; San Vicente 2001

References

Agarwal, Bina. 2001. Participatory Exclusions, Community Forestry, and Gender: An Analysis for South Asia and a Conceptual Framework. *World Development* 29: 1623–1648.

Agrawal, Arun, and Clark C. Gibson. 2001. The Role of Community in Natural Resource Conservation. In *Communities and the Environment: Ethnicity, Gender, and the State in Community-Based Conservation*. Arun Agarwal and Clark C. Gibson, eds. Pp. 1–31. New Brunswick, NJ: Rutgers University Press.

Alcala, Angel C. 2001. *Marine Reserves in the Philippines: Historical Development, Effects and Influence on Marine Conservation Policy*. Makati, Philippines: Bookmark.

Alibutud, Raul. 1993. Rough Winds Over Calancan Bay. In *Saving the Earth: The Philippine Experience*, 3rd ed. Eric Gamalinda and Sheila Coronel, eds. Pp. 69–79. Manila: Philippine Center for Investigative Journalism.

Aragon, Lorraine. 1997. Distant Processes: The Global Economy and Outer Island Development in Indonesia. In *Life and Death Matters: Human Rights and the Environment at the End of the Millennium*. Barbara Rose Johnston, ed. Pp. 26–42. Walnut Creek, CA: Altamira Press.

Arquiza, Yasmin D. 1999. *Rhythm of the Sea: Coastal Environmental Profile of San Vicente, Palawan*. Cebu City, Philippines: Coastal Resource Management Project.

Aswani, Shankar. 1999. Common Property Models of Sea Tenure: A Case Study from the Roviana and Vonavona Lagoons, New Georgia, Solomon Islands. *Human Ecology* 27: 417–453.

Austin, Rebecca L. 2003. *Environmental Movements and Fisherfolk Participation on a Coastal Frontier, Palawan Island, Philippines*. Unpublished PhD dissertation. Department of Anthropology, University of Georgia.

Bailey, Conner, and Caroline Pomeroy. 1996. Resource Dependency and Development Options in Coastal Southeast Asia. *Society and Natural Resources* 9: 191–199.

Barlett, Peggy. 1989. Introduction: Dimensions and Dilemmas of Householding. In *The Household Economy: Reconsidering the Domestic Mode of Production*. Richard W. Wilk, ed. Pp. 3–10. Boulder, CO: Westview Press.

Barrera, Alfredo. 1960. *Soil Survey of Palawan Province*. Manila: Bureau of Printing.

Bee, Ooi Jin. 1987. *Depletion of Forest Resources in the Philippines*. Singapore: Institute of Southeast Asian Studies, Field Report Series No. 18.

Bello, Walden. 1988. From Dictatorship to Elite Populism: The United States and the Philippine Crisis. In *Crisis and Confrontation: Ronald Reagan's Foreign Policy*. Morris H. Morley, ed. Totowa, NJ: Rowman and Littlefield.

BFAR. 1997. *1996 Philippines Profile*. Manila: Department of Agriculture, Bureau of Fisheries and Aquatic Resources.

Brett, John A. 2006. "We Sacrifice and Eat Less": The Structural Complexities of Microfinance Participation. *Human Organization* 65: 8–19.

Broad, Robin, with John Cavanagh. 1993. *Plundering Paradise: The Struggle for the Environment in the Philippines*. Berkeley: University of California Press.

Brown, Lester R. 1995. Nature's Limits. In *State of the World 1995*. Linda Stark, ed. Pp. 3–20. New York: W. W. Norton.

Brusco, Elizabeth E. 1995. *The Reformation of Machismo: Evangelical Conversion and Gender in Columbia*. Austin: University of Texas Press.

Buco, Benjamin V., Jr. 2006. Exports of Mineral Products Twice Higher. *Business World Research*, June 4, 2006.

Bureau of Mines and Geosciences. 1986. *Mineral Resources of Palawan*. Vol. 2 of *Geology and Mineral Resources of the Philippines*. Quezon City, Philippines: Bureau of Mines and Geosciences.

Cañete, Aloysius Ma. L. 2000. From Beach Seining to *Sapyaw* Fishing: Innovation, Competition, and Conflict Avoidance in a Municipal Fishery in Central Philippines. *Philippine Quarterly of Culture and Society* 28: 158–223.

Cavanagh, John, and Jerry Mander. 2004. *Alternatives to Economic Globalization: A Better World is Possible*. San Francisco: Brett-Kohler.

Christie, Patrick, Alan T. White, and Delma Buhat. 1994. Community-based Coral Reef Management on San Salvador Island, the Philippines. *Society and Natural Resources* 7: 103–117.

Christie, Patrick, Bonnie J. McKay, Marc L. Miller, Celia Lowe, Alan T. White, Richard Stouffle, et al. 2003. Toward Developing a Complete Understanding: A Social Science Agenda for Marine Protected Areas. *Fisheries* 28: 22–26.

Coumans, Catherine. 2002. Case Study: Marcopper Mining Corporation—Placer Dome, Inc. http://www.minesandcommunities.org/Company/marcopper1.htm

Crawford, Brian. 2002. Seaweed Farming: An Alternative Livelihood for Small-Scale Fishers? Working Paper, Coastal Resources Center, University of Rhode Island.

CRMP. 2004. *Completion Report. The Coastal Resource Management Project-Philippines, 1996–2004*. Cebu City, Philippines: Coastal Resource Management Project of the Department of Environment and Natural Resources.

Derman, Bill, and Anne Ferguson. 1994. Human Rights, Environment, and Development: The Dispossession of Fishing Communities on Lake Malawi. In *Who Pays the Price? The Sociocultural Context of Environmental Crisis*. Barbara Rose Johnston, ed. Pp. 121–127. Washington, DC: Island Press.

Din, Kadir H. 1993. Dialogue with the Hosts: An Educational Strategy Towards Sustainable Tourism. In *Tourism in Southeast Asia*. Michael Hitchcock, Victor T. King, and Michael J. G. Parnwell, eds. Pp. 327–337. London: Routledge.

Doughty, Paul L. 2005. Learn from the Past, Be Involved in the Future. *Human Organization* 64: 303–315.

Edelman, Marc, and Angelique Haugerud. 2005. Introduction: The Anthropology of Development and Globalization. In *The Anthropology of Development and Globalization: From Classical Political Economy to Contemporary Neoliberalism*. Marc Edelman and Angelique Haugerud, eds. Pp. 1–74. Malden, MA: Blackwell.

Eder, James F. 1982. *Who Shall Succeed? Agricultural Development and Social Inequality on a Philippine Frontier*. New York: Cambridge University Press.

———. 1987. *On the Road to Tribal Extinction: Depopulation, Deculturation, and Adaptive Well-being Among the Batak of the Philippines*. Berkeley: University of California Press.

———. 1999. *A Generation Later: Household Strategies and Economic Change in the Rural Philippines*. Honolulu: University of Hawai'i Press.

———. 2004. Who are the Cuyonon? Ethnic Identity in the Modern Philippines. *Journal of Asian Studies* 63: 625–647.

———. 2006. Gender Relations and Household Economic Planning in the Rural Philippines. *Journal of Southeast Asian Studies* 37: 397–413.

Elliott, Jennifer A. 2006. *An Introduction to Sustainable Development*, 3rd ed. London: Routledge.

Ervin, Alexander M. 2005. *Applied Anthropology: Tools and Perspectives for Contemporary Practice*. Boston: Pearson Education.

Fox, Robert B. 1982. *Religion and Society among the Tagbanua of Palawan Island, Philippines*. Monograph No. 9. Manila: National Museum.

Gilman, Eric L. 1997. Community Based and Multiple Purpose Protected Areas: A Model to Select and Manage Protected Areas with Lessons from the Pacific Islands. *Coastal Management* 25: 59–91.

Harper, Malcolm. 2005. Microfinance Impact, Institutions, and Issues. *Global Future*, Fourth Quarter: 6–7.

Hutchcroft, Paul. 1998. *Booty Capitalism: The Politics of Banking in the Philippines*. Ithaca, NY: Cornell University Press.

Hviding, Edvard. 1996. *Guardians of the Marovo Lagoon: Practice, Place, and Politics in Maritime Melanesia*. Honolulu: University of Hawai'i Press.

Inda, Jonathan Xavier, and Renato Rosaldo, eds. 2004. Introduction: A World in Motion. In *The Anthropology of Globalization: A Reader*. Jonathan Xavier Inda and Renato Rosaldo, eds. Pp. 1–34. Malden, MA: Blackwell.

Jacka, Jerry K. 2005. Emplacement and Millennial Expectations in an Era of Development and Globalization: Heaven and the Appeal of Christianity among the Ipili. *American Anthropologist* 107: 643–653.

Jentoft, S., B. J. McKay, and D. C. Wilson. 1988. Social Theory and Fisheries Co-management. *Marine Policy* 22: 423–436.

Johnston, Barbara Rose, ed. 1994. *Who Pays the Price? The Sociocultural Context of Environmental Crisis*. Washington, DC: Island Press.

———. 1997. *Human Rights and the Environment at the End of the Millennium*. Walnut Creek, CA: Altamira Press.

Johnston, Barbara Rose, and Daniel Jorgensen. 1994. Mineral Development, Environmental Degradation, and Human Rights: The Ok Tedi Mine, Papua New Guinea. In *Who Pays the Price? The Sociocultural Context of Environmental Crisis*. Barbara Rose Johnston, ed. Pp. 86–98. Washington, DC: Island Press.

Kerkvliet, Benedict J. 1979. Land Reform: Emancipation or Counterinsurgency? In *Marcos and Martial Law in the Philippines*. David A. Rosenberg, ed. Ithaca, NY: Cornell University Press.

Kristofersson, Dadi, and James L. Anderson. 2006. Is there a Relationship between Fishing and Farming? Interdependence of Fisheries, Animal Production, and Aquaculture. *Marine Policy* 30: 721–725.

Kühlmann, Kai J. 2002. Evaluation of Marine Reserves as Basis to Develop Alternate Livelihoods in Coastal Areas of the Philippines. *Aquaculture International* 10: 527–549.

Kummer, David M. 1992. *Deforestation in the Post-War Philippines*. Geography Research Paper No. 234. Chicago: University of Chicago Press.

———. 2005. Deforestation in the Philippines, 1950–2000. In *Muddied Waters: Historical and Contemporary Perspectives on Management of Forests and Fisheries in Island Southeast Asia*. Peter Boomgaard, David Henley, and Manon Osseweijer, eds. Leiden: KITLV Press.

Lopez, Maria Elena. 1987. The Politics of Land at Risk in a Philippine Frontier. In *Lands at Risk in the Third World: Local-level Perspectives*. Peter D. Little and Michael Horowitz, eds. Pp. 230–248. Boulder, CO: Westview Press.

Marche, Alfred. 1970. *Luzon and Palawan*. First published 1883. Translated from the French by Carmen Ojeda and Jovita Castro. Manila: Filipiniana Book Guild.

Milgram, B. Lynne. 2001. Operationalizing Microfinance: Women and Craftwork in Ifugao, Upland Philippines. *Human Organization* 60: 212–224.

Natcher, David C., and Clifford G. Hickey. 2002. Putting the Community Back into Community-based Resource Management: A Criteria and Indicators Approach to Sustainability. *Human Organization* 61: 350–363.

National Statistics Office. 2000. *Census of Population (Philippines)*. Manila: National Statistics Office.

Netting, Robert McC. 1993. *Smallholders, Householders: Farm Families and the Ecology of Intensive Subsistence Agriculture*. Stanford, CA: Stanford University Press.

Newkirk, Gary F., and Rebecca A. Rivera. 1996. Synthesis. In *Seeds of Hope: A Collection of Case Studies on Community-Based Coastal Resources Management in the Philippines*. Elmer Magsanoc Ferrer, Lenore Polotan de la Cruz, and Marife Agoncillo Domingo, eds. Pp. 195–202. Quezon City, Philippines: College of Social Work and Community Development, University of the Philippines.

Nolan, Riall. 2002. *Development Anthropology: Encountering the Real World*. Boulder, CO: Westview Press.

Novellino, Dario. 2000. Wetlands and Indigenous Rights in Palawan: A preliminary account of the status of mangroves, coral reefs, road construction and indigenous rights in Rizal municipality, southern Palawan Island (Philippines). A report of Bangsa Palawan-Philippines (BPP) and Forest Peoples Programme (FPP), Puerto Princesa City, Philippines.

PCSD. 2005. *The State of the Environment 2004, Province of Palawan, Philippines*. Puerto Princesa City, Philippines: Palawan Council for Sustainable Development.

Pollnac, Richard B., Brian R. Crawford, and Maharlina L. G. Gorospe. 2001. Discovering Factors that Influence the Success of Community-based Marine Protected Areas in the Visayas, Philippines. *Ocean & Coastal Management* 44: 683–710.

Pomeroy, Robert S., and Michael D. Pido. 1995. Initiatives Toward Fisheries Co-management in the Philippines: The Case of San Miguel Bay. *Marine Policy* 19: 213–226.

Pomeroy, Robert S., Enrique G. Oracion, Richard B. Pollnac, and Demberge A. Caballes. 2005. Perceived Economic Factors Influencing the Sustainability of Integrated Coastal Management Projects in the Philippines. *Ocean & Coastal Management* 48: 360–377.

Pomeroy, Robert S., John E. Parks, and Cristina M. Balboa. 2006. Farming the Reef: Is Aquaculture a Solution for Reducing Fishing Pressure on Coral Reefs? *Marine Policy* 30: 111–130.

Renard, Yves. 2005. The Sea is Our Garden: Coastal Resource Management and Local Governance in the Caribbean. In *Reducing Poverty and Sustaining the Environment: The Politics of Local Engagement*. Stephen Bass, Hannah Reid, David Satterthwaite, and Paul Steele, eds. Pp. 152–179. London: Earthscan.

Repetto, Robert. 1988. *The Forests for the Trees? Government Policies and the Misuse of Forest Resources*. Washington, DC: World Resources Institute.

Rigg, Jonathan. 2003. Southeast Asia: *The Human Landscape of Modernization and Development*, 2nd ed. London: Routledge.

Robertson, Roland. 1992. *Globalization: Social Theory and Global Culture*. London: Sage.

Rush, James. 1991. *The Last Tree: Reclaiming the Environment in Tropical Asia*. New York: The Asia Society.

Russell, Susan D., and Rani T. Alexander. 2000. Of Beggers and Thieves: Customary Sharing of the Catch and Informal Sanctions in a Philippine Fishery. In *State and Community in Fisheries Management: Power, Policy, and Practice*. E. P. Durrenberger and T. D. King, eds. Pp. 19–40. Westport, CT: Bergin & Garvey.

San Vicente. 2001. *Municipal Coastal Resource (CRM) Plan, 2001–2003*. San Vicente, Philippines: Municipality of San Vicente.

Smith, Stephen C. 2005. Has the Development Community Over-invested in Microfinance? *Global Future*, Fourth Quarter.

Stonich, Susan C. 1994. Producing Food for Export: Environmental Quality and Social Justice Implications of Shrimp Mariculture in Honduras. In *Who Pays the Price? The Sociocultural Context of Environmental Crisis*. Barbara Rose Johnston, ed. Pp. 110–120. Washington, DC: Island Press.

Sunderlin, W. D., and M. L. G. Gorospe. 1997. Fishers' Organizations and Modes of Co-management: The Case of San Miguel Bay, Philippines. *Human Organization* 56: 333–343.

Stoffle, Richard W., and Jessica Minnis. 2005. *Seventh Trip Report: Findings from Six Bahamian Settlements in the Exumas*. Tucson, AZ: Bureau of Applied Research in Anthropology.

STREAM. 2003. *Improving Coastal Livelihoods through Sustainable Aquaculture Practices*. Bangkok, Thailand: The STREAM Initiative, Network of Aquaculture Centres in Asia-Pacific, Kasetsart University.

Tapales, Proserpina Domingo. 1986. Assessing the Impact of Authoritarian Rule on the Philippine Government: What Efficiency? What Accountability? *Pilipinas* 6: 21–34.

Utting, Peter. 2000. An Overview of the Potential and Pitfalls of Participatory Conservation. In *Forest Policy and Politics in the Philippines*. Peter Utting, ed. Pp. 171–215. Quezon City, Philippines: Ateneo de Manila University Press.

Valientes, Rodger. 2004. Threats to Palawan Fishery: An Economic Analysis. In *Surublien: Strategies to Conserve Palawan's Biodiversity*. R. D. Anda and J. G. Tabangay-Baldera, eds. Pp. 24–27. Puerto Princesa City, Philippines: Provincial Government of Palawan.

Vitug, Marites Dañguilan. 1993. *Power from the Forest: The Politics of Logging*. Manila: Philippine Center for Investigative Journalism.

White, A. T., C. A. Courtney, and A. Salamanca. 2002. Experience with Marine Protected Areas Planning and Management in the Philippines. *Coastal Management* 30: 1–26.

Wilk, Richard W. 1991. The Household in Anthropology: Panacea or Problem? *Reviews in Anthropology* 20: 1–12.

Wolf, Diane L. 1991. Does Father Know Best? A Feminist Critique of Household Strategy Research. *Research in Rural Sociology and Development* 5: 29–43.

Yano, Takao. 1994. The Characteristics of Fisherfolk Culture in Panay: From the Viewpoint of Fishing Ground Exploitation. In *Fishers of the Visayas. Visayan Maritime Anthropological Studies I: 1991–1993*. Iwao Ushijima and Cynthia Neri Zayas, eds. Pp. 3–51. Quezon City, Philippines: College of Social Sciences and Philosophy, University of the Philippines.

Index